So here's what I want you to do, God helping you: Take your everyday, ordinary life—your sleeping, eating, going-to-work, and walking-around life—and place it before God as an offering.

The Apostle Paul, Romans 12:1 *(The Message)*

Shift 2.0

*Helping Congregations Back
into the
Game of Effective Ministry*

by Dr. Phil Maynard

Market
Square
BOOKS

Shift 2.0
Helping Congregations Back
into the
Game of Effective Ministry

by Dr. Phil Maynard

©2018 Market Square Publishing Company, LLC.
books@marketsquarebooks.com
P.O. Box 23664   Knoxville, Tennessee 37933

ISBN:1732309221- ISBN: 978-1-7323092-2-7

Library of Congress: 2018946905

Printed and Bound in the United States of America

Editor: Kristin Lighter
Cover Illustration ©2018 Market Square Publishing, LLC

Table of Contents

Dedication

It was a great joy to walk into a gathering of Conference leaders and find a District Superintendent reading a copy of *Shift*. Also, it has been touching to have conversations with pastors around the country where they talked about using Shift as a resource for their leadership teams.

By all accounts, the first edition of *Shift* has been found to be a helpful resource for churches seeking to find their way forward in an ever-changing world.

With this second edition (updated and expanded), I have endeavored to make this resource even more practical and helpful to church leaders—local, district, and conference. With new content, surveys, and lots of examples of effective ministry, it is my prayer that churches will be inspired, encouraged, and most of all resourced to move into God's preferred future.

As always, the presentation of this resource is stronger because of the detailed review by my wife, Becky. It is better because of her attention to detail. So am I.

Dr. Phil Maynard

Foreword

by Paul Nixon

I have consulted with hundreds of churches in the last few years—and so it is no small thing for me to say that *Shift* is relevant to every single one of those churches. All of them. This is the first book I have run across in some time about which I can say this.

When my colleague Phil Maynard first told me about the manuscript he was writing (in a Popeye's Restaurant in Jacksonville, Florida earlier this year), I listened carefully to the five major shifts that he was proposing. I told him, "You nailed it. Those are the shifts." In an era where everyone has a different angle and prescription for how to fix ailing churches, rarely do we see a resource that really cuts to the bottom line. Phil has identified the key shifts that all churches must make if they are to have a fruitful ministry in the next decade. Rural, urban, black, Hispanic, Anglo, Asian, multicultural, liberal, evangelical—they all need to think through these key shifts and figure out a path forward in ministry in sync with each.

When I finally got my hands on the manuscript and started reading, the first thing that went through my mind was not some floundering church with which I am consulting, but rather the new church launch team with which I am working in my hometown. In other words, the key concepts and practices outlined in *Shift* are just as relevant to a brand-new church as to a church that is seeking to renew its ministry. The reason for this is because so often the leaders in new churches bring along baggage from the Twentieth Century church.

A few of you may lead missional churches—and you may totally get the shift from Serve-us to Service. But my coaching group works with enough missional churches to know that most of them have to work constantly at moving forward in terms of biblical hospitality and calling people to depth of discipleship.

You may think your church has its act together and does not need any coaching. Careful there! For many effective churches, Phil Maynard's suggested shifts will unpack and bring clarity to key shifts they have already made. Nonetheless, all growing churches constantly experience the temptation to get lazy because their ministry is thriving. When we get lazy, we tend to fall back into old habits and ways of thinking.

Most twenty-first century churches, however, are neither new nor missional nor effective in reaching people with the gospel. That's just the truth of the matter. Most of our churches are stuck, declining, aging and struggling in various ways. *Shift* is written most explicitly for the church that thought they had ministry figured out 30 years ago, but where nothing today is working as well as it used to work. If this is the case in the place that you call church, I encourage you to buy up a box full of copies of *Shift* and to get your church's leaders thinking through each of these key movements.

It would not hurt for all of your church's leaders to read the whole book. But then you can divide it up by areas of ministry responsibility and invite one group to really dig into the chapter on hospitality (which, I might add, is the best and most comprehensive thing I have read on that subject since I picked up a copy of Nouwen's *Reaching Out* in 1979). A group that leads worship can dig into that chapter. And so forth. I cannot imagine any ministry team wasting their time on this—the discussions, the ah-ha's, the practical improvements to ministry are almost guaranteed to any ministry team that seriously engages *Shift!*

Thank you, Phil Maynard, for giving us this immensely practical book—as we dig into its pages, you provide us more than good theory: you coach us and suggest to us excellent resources. I celebrate all of the shifts that are about to speed up in churches all over North America because they get their hands on these pages.

Paul Nixon

- Author of several popular books, including **We Refuse to Lead a Dying Church** and **The Surprise Factor**
- Leader of Epicenter Group
- National consultant and coach for congregations in redevelopment and for new church plants
- New Church Strategist for Path 1 (New Church Start Division of the General Board of Discipleship, United Methodist Church).

Introduction

Picture the scene in Ezekiel 37. Imagine God in a valley leading the prophet back and forth among broken, brittle bones—a place no Jew wants to be. Then God asks, "Can these bones live?" The situation must have looked hopeless to Ezekiel, but he replies, "Sovereign Lord, you alone know." Then God commands him to prophesy to the bones and, when he obeys, a miracle occurs. It starts as a noise, a rattling sound, as the bones come together. God attaches the tendons and then covers the skeletons with skin. Then from the four winds, God breathes life into those dry bones, and they stand on their feet, ready to occupy the land and be a force for God.

While Ezekiel's vision was intended to bring hope to the Jewish exiles following their capture by King Nebuchadnezzar of Babylon, that Scripture passage is still a powerful image today. It is a reminder of God's power to restore.

Look around you. Where are you seeing the fresh wind of God's Spirit breathe new life into dry, brittle bones?

As a church consultant and denominational leader, I am witnessing God breathe new life into churches with whom I have worked. Congregations are making the Shift—actually a series of individual shifts that, when combined together, shift the culture of their churches—bringing vitality and fruitfulness. These individual shifts include:

- From *Fellowship* to *Hospitality*

- From *Worship as an Event* to *Worship as a Lifestyle*

- From *Membership* to *Discipleship*

- From *"Serve Us"* to *Service*

- From a *"Survival Mentality"* to *Extravagant Generosity*.

I am writing this book because I believe that every church has the potential to be vital and fruitful. These are not just buzzwords. They are words filled with hope and promise.

Not every church will choose to live into this potential.

We all know of churches that have made the decision to circle the wagons, hang on to their revered traditions, focus on the contentment of 'members,' and ignore the world around them. If this is your church, or a church you are working with or trying to coach to health, this material may not be for you.

Instead, if the church has the will to move into a more vital ministry, this material is full of great ideas to help you do that. It is not easy. This Shift will require much of you. It will challenge some of your long-held assumptions about what effective ministry looks like. It will require letting go of some things that may have been held dear for a lifetime. Accordingly, it will engage the most creative parts of your being to apply clear principles to your particular circumstances.

Each church will need to take the concepts, tools, and practices to figure out how they best work in its distinctive context. Questions have been provided to help leaders and coaches lead their congregations in meaningful conversation about where they are and where they want to go.

Dr. Phil Maynard
Founder and CEO, Excellence in Ministry Coaching (EMC3)

Shift 1

From Fellowship to Hospitality

"My command is this: Love each other
as I have loved you."

—Jesus, John 15:12

Life is not about stuff we own or accumulate. It is not even
about personal accomplishment. Life is about people. We
can replace stuff, but we can't replace people!

—Michael Slaughter, *Momentum for Life*[1]

As a school for love, the church becomes a congregation
where people learn from one another how to love.

—Bishop Robert Schnase, *Five Practices of Fruitful Congregations*[2]

Congregational Survey

At the beginning of each chapter, a congregational survey is included. Each of these surveys is a diagnostic tool to help you bridge the gap between assumptions and reality. You can't begin making a shift if you don't have a clear-eyed view of your starting point.

For instance, if you ask a general question like, "Are you a friendly and welcoming congregation," people will inevitably respond, "Yes!" It is only through asking detailed questions about congregational habits that deeper truths are revealed.

This chapter's survey can be completed by leadership and congregation members to evaluate the quality of hospitality within your church. After reading the statement to the left, rate your response from 1-4 with 4 representing strong agreement and 1 representing disagreement. (Feel free to reproduce the survey from these pages or visit the Excellence in Ministry Coaching website for a printable version.)

	From Fellowship to Hospitality	1	2	3	4
1.	Visitors are engaged in conversation by a participant in worship seeking to learn about them and their needs.				
2.	Most members have a close friend or group of friends who are regular participants in the worship and discipleship activities of this congregation.				
3.	This congregation attracts people from a variety of cultural groups and provides a place where all feel welcome.				
4.	This congregation is actively involved in the life of the immediately surrounding community, making a difference and friends in the process.				

		1	2	3	4
5.	Following worship, the church provides an easily visible space with refreshments and encourages participants to invite someone new to join them for fellowship.				
6.	The people in this congregation put relationships above whatever issues might be divisive.				
7.	Worship leadership provides training and actively encourages participants to engage those who may be new or unknown.				
8.	When someone misses worship for more than two consecutive week-ends, there is someone who makes contact.				
9.	Following the first visit to our worship, the person/family receives a brief visit and a welcome gift from a lay person.				
10.	When someone has been in worship three or more weeks, they are invited into a relationship with a sponsor/guide to help them get connected in a meaningful way.				
11.	Following the second visit, a newcomer is invited to participate in a 'get to know you' interview with the pastor.				
12.	By not asking people to introduce themselves, our congregation avoids putting people on the spot during the worship welcome time.				
13.	Our facilities are clean and free of clutter for weekly worship experiences.				
14.	We offer some form of informational meeting at the conclusion of worship for those who would like to know more about the ministry of the congregation.				
15.	Our congregation offers a first class nursery during worship with trained staff, bright and clean facilities, sanitized toys, and a parent notification system.				

		1	2	3	4
16.	Our church website is attractive, full of stories, up-to-date, and provides easy access to pertinent information about worship (including directions).				
17.	This church offers a variety of attractional events and programs to introduce people in the community to our ministries.				
18.	We encourage our leaders and members to actively engage in networking with friends, neighbors, relatives, and associates to build relationships and introduce them to Jesus.				
19.	We actively support the invitational process by providing attractive, professional quality invitations to special events, sermon series, and seasonal emphases.				
20.	Our congregation is actively engaged in the life of the community, building relationships and sharing the love of Christ.				
21.	We have a system for engaging worship participants, particularly newcomers, in small groups or other discipleship partnering relationships.				
22.	We train our members and regular attenders in the basics of conflict management.				
23.	There is a system in place for providing pastoral care for our members that includes lay participation and leadership.				
24.	Our communication tools (bulletins, flyers, newsletters, postcards, etc.) are of professional quality and avoid insider language.				
25.	We encourage and celebrate the development of relationships beyond the congregation, making this a priority over attending church activities.				

A perfect score on this survey would be 100 points.

When using this with your leadership team or congregation, here is how you determine an average score:

Total the points for each individual survey. Add the points from all the individual surveys together. Divide that total number by the number of surveys that were completed. This gives you an average score (out of 100 possible points), providing you with a "grade" for your congregational health in this area. Using a standard academic scale:

$$90+ \quad = \quad A$$
$$80\text{-}89 \quad = \quad B$$
$$70\text{-}79 \quad = \quad C$$
$$60\text{-}69 \quad = \quad D$$

What grade does your hospitality receive? What did the survey reveal? What is your strongest area? What do you hope for in hospitality? Write your answers in the space below:

Consider the following. It's a familiar story lived out in many congregations across the United States:

> **Someone is in crisis—a couple has their first child, or a family moves to the area. They decide to attend the church down the street. They don't know anyone, so they arrive late and slip into the back row of seats. Because the bulletin is geared to the congregation, they struggle to keep up with what is going on. During "moments of friendliness," a few people nod at them, but most of the congregation visits with each other. After the service, someone points them in the direction of the Fellowship Hall, where there is coffee, but then leaves them. Once they find their way to the refreshments table, they end up standing on their own. It would be no different if they attended a small group or Sunday school class. The people in the church have known each other so long that it would be difficult to break in. They don't know the stories, the history, the people.**

How do you react to this account? How does it make you feel? No wonder so few are coming to know the love of Jesus! People are not seeing it lived out, even in the one place that they would expect to find it.

Hospitality is more than fellowship with one another. It's about opening our hearts to others and building relationships, plain and simple. Let's consider some observations about hospitality in the local congregation based on current research and my work with congregations in transformation:

- Depending on the study referenced, somewhere between 60–80% of people who visit a congregation come because they were personally invited.

- As a general rule, in most communities 50% or less of the population is participating in the life of any church congregation.

- Most people who visit a congregation decide within the first

10 minutes or less following arrival on the church campus whether or not they will return. This, of course, is long before the pastor preaches and sometimes even before the music starts!

- The driving factor in the decision to return is often the personal connections made by members of the congregation—interactions beyond those with the greeters or pastor.

- People are more engaged in the life of the congregation if they have a good friend who is also involved.

- The follow-up with first-time visitors and with those who have missed a couple of consecutive weeks in worship is a key factor in maintaining the relationship.

- Hospitality is a significant dimension of Christian discipleship and can be developed through intentional discipleship training.

- Hospitality is bigger than how one is welcomed to the worship event. It is part of a larger system of discipleship that includes friendships, intentional discipleship relationships, witnessing, and more.

- Hospitality includes both personal and congregational dimensions, and these are interrelated. Each supports the other.

When coaching the local congregation in the area of hospitality, all of these observations come into play. The goal is to help the congregation consider how to increase the relational level of its ministry. Perhaps the first question to consider is why such relational development matters from a theological perspective.

A Theology of Hospitality

Before we dig too deeply into the practical matters of moving toward excellence in the ways we offer hospitality, it needs to be clear why the shift from fellowship to hospitality is so important. Why are we to practice hospitality from a theological perspective? Isn't it enough that we gather with people who are like us and whose company makes us feel good? Aren't we called to love each other, care for each other, and enjoy each other?

The Bible is pretty clear that this isn't enough!

In fact, from the charge of Abram, "I will bless you . . . and you will be a blessing . . . and all peoples on earth will be blessed through you" (Genesis 12:2–3), to the charge from Jesus to "[G]o and make disciples of all nations, baptizing them . . . and teaching them" (Matthew 28:19–20), to the vision offered to John in Revelation that "They will be his people, and God himself will be with them and be their God . . . the old order of things has passed away . . . I am making everything new" (Revelation 21: 3–5), it is clear that the work of God is not limited to the fellowship of existing believers.

While hospitality in our contemporary culture has taken the form of 'fellowship' where we welcome friends to our table, in the biblical tradition hospitality was focused on welcoming the stranger. This includes those with the physical needs of shelter and nourishment, but also those who know the pain of exclusion. Jesus himself modeled this as those who turned to him found welcome and the promise of being included in the Kingdom of God. Not only did he urge his followers to generously welcome those in need, but he also promised that these acts of kindness were personally experienced by the Son of Man himself. This is related in Matthew 25 when he says, "The King will reply, 'Truly I tell you, whatever you did for one of the least of these brothers and sisters of mine, you did for me.'"

It's not just about us!

The driving force behind the building of relationships is the expression of God's grace (unmerited love) through the acceptance of all persons as being those God loves and the invitation for all to discover the fullness of that love for themselves. It is a grace that flows from the center of our own experience of God's love, and it is meant to extend from us to all people. People are accepted wherever they are in the flow of God's love and invited to discover the depths of God's love through the growth of relationships with other believers and the growth of a personal relationship with Jesus Christ.

We love because we have been loved. We welcome others because we have been welcomed. We invite others to discover this grace because of what we have learned for ourselves about the transforming power of God's love.

This relational dimension is the engine that drives our witness in the community and world, our worship as the body of Christ, and our growth in maturity as disciples of Jesus Christ.

Let's consider a simple diagram to explain the 'big picture' approach to hospitality:

Dimensions of Hospitality

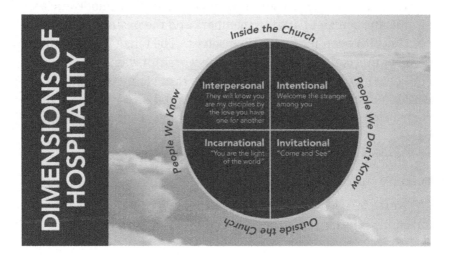

Refers to the level and quality of relational connections
within the congregation, the people we know.

Guiding Principle

**The level of engagement by any person in the life and
ministry of a local congregation is largely determined by
the level of relational connections they experience.**

Key to all the dimensions of hospitality is that of interpersonal hospitality. This is all about meaningful connections at all
points in the discipleship flow of a congregation. For example, I
worked with a congregation that had been in crisis mode due to a
simmering conflict between members and the pastor, as well as
conflicts between members themselves. The tension in any gathering of this congregation (including worship) was so thick you
could cut it with a knife. The amazing thing to me was that they
couldn't understand why people who showed up for worship in
their beautiful 100-year-old sanctuary didn't seem to ever come
back!

How we treat each other also shows up in the way others
perceive our connection with them.

At the heart of the Christian faith journey is the idea of
authentic relationships.

- We are called to be in relationship with God (Father, Son,
  and Holy Spirit).

- We are called to be in relationship with each other (modeling
  the relationship in which our Trinitarian God lives).

- We are called to be in relationship with those outside of the
  church.

Graphically, these concepts are represented by three parts of
the same whole:

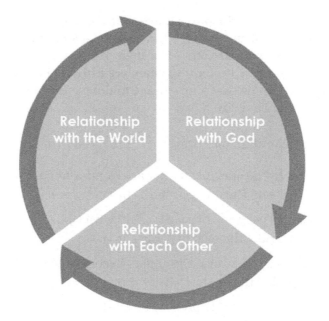

As each portion is strengthened, so is the next, and so also is the whole. I want to suggest five benefits of strong interpersonal hospitality:

- **Synergy:** Power and energy that comes from spiritual friendships
- **Motivation:** Challenge and influence to keep growing in our relationship with God
- **Encouragement:** Bringing comfort, consolation, and counsel to one another
- **Accountability:** Objective counsel and helpful challenge
- **Support:** People to come alongside us and help us keep moving forward.

In John 17:20–23, Jesus offers this prayer for believers:

> I pray also for those who will believe in me through their message, that all of them may be one, Father, just as you are in me and I am in you. May they also be in

us so that the world may believe that you have sent me. I have given them the glory that you gave me, that they may be one as we are one—I in them and you in me—so that they may be brought to complete unity. Then the world will know that you sent me and have loved them even as you have loved me.

There are several themes present in just these three verses:

1. That to "be one, just as you are in me and I am in you" reflects on the unity of the Trinity.

2. That as we grow in relationship with God ("be in us"), the world will come to believe in Jesus.

3. That we (believers) can in fact become one with each other as fully as the Trinity is one.

4. That it is Jesus' expressed desire that we experience unity as believers.

5. That our witness to the world depends on the kind of relationships we build.

There are several very practical considerations when it comes to living in authentic relationship with each other as disciples of Jesus:

Forgiveness: Jesus said, "Blessed are the peacemakers" (Matthew 5:9). Paul said, "If it is possible, as far as it depends on you, live at peace with everyone" (Romans 12:18). **How do you relate to people with whom you do not agree or who have hurt you?** Jesus said that even sinners are nice to those who like and affirm them. "Love your enemies" (Matthew 5:44). "Bless those who curse you, pray for those who mistreat you" (Luke 6:28). Make peace with those who have hurt you. Our culture is strong on individual rights, on stressing what we deserve and on what we are entitled to in relationships. Jesus turned much of this thinking upside down and said to those for whom he died 'while we were yet sinners,' "Love each other as I have loved you" (John 15:12).

Acceptance: How do you relate to and welcome those who are different than you? In nature, "birds of a feather flock together." However, in the Kingdom of God, everyone is welcomed. This was hard for the early church to hear, but the Holy Spirit expanded the early church's understanding of the inclusiveness of the Kingdom story by story, as if a bulldozer were knocking down every cultural barrier that kept people apart. Could sinners be welcomed? Could tax collectors and prostitutes? Could Greek-speaking Jews? Could Gentile God-fearers? Could Roman soldiers? Could godless Gentiles? Could those who had been worshiping foreign gods? The answer repeatedly was "Yes!" God's welcome includes even them. Yet the early church struggled to welcome all these different people into their table fellowship. **Who might not feel welcomed by you into your small group, or who might feel uncomfortable kneeling beside you taking communion?** Jesus seemed purposefully to hang out with people who were not like him. What's more, they seemed to be drawn to his company. **When you hang out with people not like you, are they drawn to you?**

Accountability: The Apostle Paul scatters throughout his letters a series of admonitions, known as the "one anothers," that provide insight into how we are called to do life together. A central theme in these "one anothers" is that of accountability, expressed in a variety of ways: submit to one another, encourage one another, admonish one another, bear with one another, agree with one another, live in harmony with one another. Life as a disciple of Jesus Christ is lived in accountable relationships. This idea is also at the heart of the Methodist movement begun by John Wesley. Community and authentic relationships were supported through Class Meetings by a high level of accountability using a Covenant of Discipleship.

Congregations that develop a strong sense of interpersonal hospitality help create safe places and safe people. Unlike "abandoners" who start a relationship but can't finish it, "critics" who take on a parental role (telling you what to do), or "irresponsibles" who don't take care of themselves or follow through on their commitments to others, safe people are trustworthy people. In their book, *Safe People*, Henry Cloud and John Townsend describe a safe relationship as one that does three things: (1) Draws us closer to God (Matt. 22:37–38), (2) Draws us closer to others (Matt. 22:39), and (3) Helps us become the real person God created us to be (Eph. 2:10).[3]

There are many ways to develop safe places and safe people in your congregation.

Make small group ministries a centerpiece of congregational life. Moving people from the relative anonymity of sitting in the worship pews to engaging others in a small group setting is probably the most significant thing a congregation can do to foster the development of strong interpersonal hospitality. Small groups foster the development of deep friendships, invite us to engage our faith journey more fully, encourage maturity in our spiritual journey, and provide what may be the best forum for caring for the needs of one another.

Teach the "one anothers." The New Testament is full of instructions in the form of "one another" statements about how to live in right relationship with your fellow disciples, as well as the practice of interpersonal hospitality. A listing of these "one anothers" is found in Appendix A. An excellent resource for small group study around this theme is Jim Van Yperen's *Authentic Community* curriculum based on the "one another" statements.

Train the congregation in appropriate ways to deal with conflict. Conflict is an inevitable part of being in community. People will always have differing opinions and perspectives, their own agendas, and issues of control and power. How we deal with those is what makes Christian community unique. There are several resources to assist the local congregation in dealing with conflict in a biblical manner. I want to suggest two that I have found helpful:

- Peacemaker Ministries: Provides a variety of small group training materials. This organization also trains persons in conflict coaching, mediation, and conflict resolution.

- Making Peace Ministry: Provides a variety of small group training materials and has trained coaches and mediators available to work with congregations in conflict situations.

Provide training in caring for one another. Many congregations train ministry team leaders, small group leaders, and pastoral care teams in the basic skills of caring for others in a variety of life situations. An excellent resource for this training is Stephen Ministries, which provides 50 hours of training to equip people to provide care to those experiencing difficult life situations.

Build a congregational behavioral covenant. A behavioral covenant is an agreement composed to clarify how members and leaders of a congregation will behave toward one another. It is a fairly common practice for leadership teams to develop a behavioral covenant for their work together, and it is becoming more common for congregations to follow this practice as well.

The key to a behavioral covenant is that it specifies the actual behaviors or ways that people will treat each other. For example, rather than saying "we will respect each other," the behavior might be "we will show respect for each other by listening to and seeking to understand the other person's point of view."

The behavioral covenant becomes the standard by which we do life together.

To support the development of behavioral covenants, Excellence in Ministry Coaching offers a free PowerPoint, titled "Behavioral Covenants: Holy Manners," found under the "resources" tab, "hospitality" section, at emc3coaching.com.

Getting Started

It is almost impossible to overstate the value of building relationships within the congregation. We assume that people come to church to meet God. This is certainly true. Yet, the thing that will keep people engaged at your church is not the quality of the worship experience or the stained-glass windows or the amazing music ministry.

It is the relationships they develop.

A general rule related to the importance of these connections is that people need to be part of at least six relationships—stated succinctly, they need to make six new friends—within the first six months at the church, or they are likely to drop out and try somewhere else. There is a direct correlation between the number of friendships developed and continued involvement in the church.

So, how can your congregation help foster these friendships? You might consider the following:

- Utilize your hospitality center as a connecting point with hosts/hostesses. They should be trained to connect the new people they meet with other people it would be good for them to get to know (e.g. people with similar interests, leaders in the congregation, or families with the same age children).

- Host gathering events (e.g. men's breakfast, women's Bible study, or outside speakers) with opportunities for people to gather at table groups and engage in conversation.

- Provide Connect Groups. These are groups formed around the needs and interests of participants. They do not have to be 'churchy' in nature! They could include these kinds of interest-based groups:

  ○ Biking
  ○ Quilting
  ○ Sewing
  ○ Bowling
  ○ Hiking
  ○ Fishing
  ○ Golfing
  ○ Book clubs
  ○ Investing
  ○ Kayaking
  ○ Cooking.

- Provide a variety of short-term study groups, including Bible studies, exploration of social issues, and skills development classes (e.g. parenting skills, job hunting skills).

- Provide service groups focused on meeting particular needs in the local community.

- Consider a "Dinner for Eight" program. Everybody likes to eat, and most people enjoy getting together for dinner with someone else. Why not have this happen in a way that encourages and supports the building of relationships? Dinners for Eight could happen with eight individuals or four couples and either in someone's home or at a local restaurant. With a little support from the church, this could happen in a way that connects people that have previously been in such a relationship with other folks from the congregation.

- Leverage opportunities to serve in the church. Invite people that are new or have not been very involved to serve with other members in the church.

One final note on interpersonal relationships. The building of relationships is greatly enhanced as people are encouraged to share their stories. In every setting (study groups, committees, Dinners for Eight, and even worship) provide ways for participants to share their life journeys and how God has been at work. For a fuller treatment of this idea, see my book, *Connect!*[4]

Questions for Leaders and Coaches
Related to Interpersonal Hospitality

How are relationships encouraged and supported?

What is the system for engaging participants in small groups or other discipleship partnering relationships (e.g. mentoring, coaching, spiritual friends)? What is the track record in the congregation for moving people from worship to connections with small groups or other forms of discipleship?

What is the level of conflict within the congregation? What type of training is made available to encourage healthy conflict management?

How do members of this congregation provide care for one another? How might they be encouraged to do so?

What is the system for following up with regular worshipers who have been absent for two or more weeks?

Intentional Hospitality

Refers to the practices of members and the congregation in making relational connections with people they don't know who are visiting and/or returning.

Guiding Principle

People who visit a church return and/or stay connected because they are engaged as friends and feel like they could fit into this congregation.

Intentional hospitality has two primary objectives:

- To provide relational connections when newcomers join in worship.
- To set an example for disciples in the way they might live beyond the church walls.

I attended a church a while back that has become very intentional about extending hospitality to those who come for the first time. When I arrived at the front door of the church, I was welcomed by a greeter who shook my hand. Then an usher welcomed me and handed me a bulletin for worship. During the morning announcements, welcome was extended by the pastor, and visitors were asked to stand, introduce themselves, and be welcomed by the congregation. An usher came and handed me a welcome packet with information about the congregation, a visitor information card, and a visitor nametag to wear. During the greeting time, several people shook my hand and said "welcome to worship." Following the worship service, the pastor shook my hand as I exited the sanctuary. Also, in the week following my visit to this church, I received a form letter from the pastor thanking me for visiting and expressing the hope that I would return.

My experience describes the more typical approaches of congregations in welcoming visitors or 'guests,' which is a term I prefer. Language is important. A visitor is someone who is with you on a temporary basis. There is no expectation that they will be engaged in a long-term relationship. A guest is different. Guests are welcomed into our homes. We prepare our homes to receive them. We are intentional about offering hospitality in ways that make guests feel comfortable and part of the family.

To be perfectly blunt, in many congregations the intentional practices described above would be a major step forward in offering hospitality. I recently visited six United Methodist congregations within a 10-mile radius of my home. Not one of them invited me to a hospitality center for refreshments (although all had such a center in place), offered information about the church, or sent even a form letter welcoming me to the church. No one called to say hello or dropped off a welcome gift. Yet, these basic hospitality responses are what I call 'platform level' practices. If they are missing (e.g. greeters or ushers, etc.) it is a red flag for guests. These basics are expected as standard practice. Doing them doesn't automatically make people feel welcome, but not doing them can make people feel unwelcome. Here are some of the primary platform level practices:

- Parking lot greeters
- Entryway greeters (at all entry points)
- Ushers
- Congregational greeting
- Connect cards / pew pads
- Information packets
- Follow-up letter / phone call.

Of course, we should be thoughtful about each of these practices. Otherwise, some of them can inadvertently work against us. For example, when asked about the greeting time that is standard practice in most churches, a sizable majority of people have indicated that they would prefer not to be publicly recognized (embarrassed) by having to stand and/or introduce themselves. This shouldn't surprise us. Think about some of the greatest fears people have:

• Going to a party with strangers

• Having to speak before a crowd

• Being asked personal questions in public.

When people show up for the first time in worship, they are automatically thinking things like, "Do I fit in here?" and "Did people like me?"

There are a variety of factors at play in how people get the answers to those questions. For example, in a congregation on the east coast of Florida, all the standard intentional hospitality expressions are in place (greeters, ushers, pastoral welcome), but this congregation goes beyond these common expressions of congeniality. Regular participants in the congregational life who have the gift of hospitality seek out newcomers and engage them in conversation, working to learn about the newcomers and their needs. If appropriate, they sit with the newcomers during worship. Following worship, these hosts invite their new friends to join them at the hospitality center for refreshments and conversation. At the hospitality center, the new friends are introduced to other regulars, relevant staff, and the pastor. These expressions of hospitality were already exceptional in our experience, but then these hosts did something completely unexpected. They invited their new acquaintances to join them for lunch at a local restaurant, so that they might have the opportunity to get to know each other better!

As you might imagine, most people experiencing this level of welcome immediately feel like they fit in quite well.

I mentioned a hospitality center in the example above. It is one of the key ways that a church can support the making of connections. The hospitality center needs to be in a prominent location (not over in the fellowship hall) and have refreshments available for people as they gather to connect. Having regulars trained to invite newcomers to join them for some refreshments is important, as is having them introduce newcomers to other regular attenders, staff, and the pastor. It is also important to get guest names for purposes of follow-up. It was the practice in the last congregation I served to close the service with this invitation: "If you are sitting close to someone you don't know or don't know well, invite them to join you at the hospitality center for some refreshments and conversation. Make a new friend today! This is an important part of our worship together."

In the previous example, the hosts invited guests to lunch to get to know them better. More common, but still exceptional, is the approach of taking a welcome gift (bread, pie, homemade jellies, etc.) to the home of a newcomer within 24 hours of their initial visit. This is a quick visit just to drop off the gift and express a warm welcome. Doug Anderson, quoting Herb Miller in *The Race to Reach Out,* suggests, "Be brief, be bright [positive], and be gone."[5] Opportunities to 'sell' the church will come later. The timing of this visit is important. Waiting longer than 24 hours dramatically reduces the impact. However, it is true that not all communities respond well to a porch visit as described above. Anderson makes these additional observations:

- The more urban the area, the larger the church, and the younger the guest (under 45), the more valued a phone call.

- The more rural the area, the smaller the church, and the older (over 55) the guest, the more valued a visit.[6]

For follow-up visits to be accomplished, the church must have the names of those who visited. Getting this information can be accomplished in several ways:

1. Have members write the name down as part of their conversation with newcomers.

2. Have guests complete a "connect card" or sign in on pew pads (which only works if members also complete this information).

3. Review checks placed in the offering for names of those that are not regular attenders.

The question is often raised about how to get people to complete the "connect cards." Here are some suggestions:

- Most congregations find that the "connect card" (see sample below) is a more effective way to get information than traditional pew pads utilized to collect attendance information.

- Invite everyone in attendance to complete the card, not just the guests.

- Pass the cards down the row and encourage people to notice the names of those nearby.

- Have a member present a warm welcome, perhaps even sharing something about why they love the church.

- Explain exactly what you want them to do with the "connect card" and then ask them to fill it out.

- Share why it would be helpful to the worship participants (including the regular participants) to provide the information you are requesting.

Grace Connect Card

today's date _____

email: _____

☐ 1st time guest   ☐ 2nd time guest
☐ regular attendee ☐ member

full name _____

address _____

city/state/zip _____

birthday _____/_____/_____

phone:

    home _____

    work _____

    cell _____

☐ check here if: address change, phone or family updates (Please write updates in feedback section on back)

new to Grace?
how did you hear about us?
☐ friend   ☐ online
☐ other _____

As an added incentive for first-time guests to fill out the "connect card," a couple of churches I am aware of offer to make a charitable donation of $10 to an organization supported by the congregation. This is, of course, a win-win-win. The charity is supported, and the guests feel good about making a difference. Meanwhile, the congregation gets contact information from the guests, making it possible to do appropriate follow-up.

Another key for intentional hospitality is a connecting interview with newcomers. This is arranged after the second visit and is usually done by the pastor. The pastor should call to set up a time (about 45 minutes long) to meet in the home of the newcomer. The purpose of the visit is to get to know them. This is a time to get accurate information about the family/individual (spelling of names, ages of children, schools attended, occupation, etc.). Even more important is the opportunity to discover how newcomers might be connected to existing small groups or to opportunities for service. The pastor does not make these connections ('sell' the groups, ministries, and programs), but passes along information to group and ministry leaders. I cannot stress enough the importance of this "getting to know you" session.

One of the preferred outcomes of this connecting interview is getting the guest/family connected with a sponsor. Some churches call them mentors or faith guides, but whatever we call them, the purpose of a sponsor is to journey with the newcomers until they reach a point of commitment to membership. The sponsor might help them find the right program support for their children, get connected in some form of small group, sit with them in worship, connect them with other church members with whom they share an affinity, and even stand with them as they join the congregation.

In a recent coaching call with a pastor serving a church that was about a year old, he described a setting of 40 to 50 people who gathered for worship on a regular basis. However, his description was of a congregation that changed every week! New people would come and might return weeks or months later, while some might never return at all. If the people who visited off-and-on were there on a more consistent basis, the weekly worship attendance would have been nearly double the current average.

What questions might you have asked this pastor if you were coaching him? (Write them in the blank space below.)

As I helped this pastor explore this congregation's regular hospitality practices, it became clear that while guests were greeted by the pastor following worship, and a gift was delivered to guests following their visit (although typically four to five days later), there was no real connection made with the congregation. There was no "getting to know you" type of conversation, so people had to figure out how to get connected on their own. In fact, the next level of engagement at this church was straight to what they termed a newcomers' class—actually a membership class.

A tweaking of regular practices, with an emphasis on the pastor making a real connection through an extended conversation, immediately began to turn this situation around.

31

As a general rule, a healthy congregation needs to have as many guests in worship over the course of a year as it has in average weekly worship attendance. Congregations are encouraged to track participation of guests. An average return rate for most congregations is about 15%. Appropriate follow-up with guests increases this percentage, and there are specific strategies proven to boost return rates:

- Following the first visit, the guest(s) would receive a handwritten note from a member welcoming them to the church. The pastor would send a letter of welcome focused on making a significant connection. If appropriate in your context, a porch visit is conducted within 48 hours, offering a welcome gift. A text might be sent later in the week expressing that you are looking forward to seeing them again in worship.

- Following the second visit, the guest(s) would receive another note from a member. The pastor would arrange for a "connecting interview." A sponsor would be assigned.

A colleague of mine, Jim Ozier, wrote a really great book about hospitality, titled *Clip In* (built around a bicycle metaphor). One of the things he recommends is that the church be careful about the messaging of the letter of welcome. He suggests that there are two different types of messaging, called 'consumer' and 'producer' approaches. You can see the contrast between them in the samples below:

Dear _____ ,

We are so glad you joined us for worship last Sunday! Here at Christ Church we have the joy of experiencing inspiring music, uplifting messages, and great fellowship every week! I hope you sensed the warmth and fellowship of our church and will come again soon.

As you can see, we have many outstanding programs for children, youth, and adults – something to meet your needs no matter where you are in your faith journey.

If you have any questions, or if we can help you in any way, please don't hesitate to contact us. I look forward to getting better acquainted in the days ahead.

In Christ's name,

_____

This first example was the "consumer" approach. The second example is different, what Jim calls the "producer" approach:

Dear_____,

Thank you for being in worship at Christ Church last week! We know it's a big step to get up on Sunday morning and go to a new church for the first time. Thanks again!

I hope your presence indicates you have a passion for making a difference in the community and in the world. Then again, maybe you have something going on in your life and you are looking for answers, or you may have been in worship for some other reason altogether. Whatever the reason, we hope that you benefited from the effort you made to be here.

Within the next few days you'll be contacted about ways you can put your passion, talents, and skills to work for the glory of God, if you have that interest at this point in your life. You'll hear about ways that can make a lasting impact and match who you are and where you are in your spiritual journey.

I hope you enjoyed your experience and will tell a friend about it. If you have any questions, please don't hesitate to text or call me at _____.

Thanks again,

_____

(Used by permission of Jim Ozier [7])

It's about what we are trying to accomplish. Are we just looking for more people to consume our services? Or do we hope to encourage people to discover the joy of making a difference? Words matter!

It is recommended that some form of continuing communication with newcomers be conducted over a period of at least six weeks. Too often, we let potential members slip through the cracks by not being intentional with our follow-up. Guest care is not a one-time thing. The following graphic from the Text In Church organization illustrates what this follow-up schedule could look like.[8]

The end goal of hospitality is that people become disciples of Jesus and engaged in the life of the congregation. I recommend that this engagement take place at three points in the congregational life: worship, a small group or other accountable relationship, and some form of service.

The vital point here is that regular attenders of the congregation engage those who are newcomers in ways that make them feel really welcomed. Notice that I am saying regular attenders and not the pastor. It is meaningful when regular people make the effort to welcome others. Not so much for the pastor—he/she gets paid to do that! Some excellent resources are available for training your church in how to be a welcoming congregation through the United Methodist Rethink Church materials.

We have discussed the essential nature of platform level hospitality experiences (which in and of themselves do not produce a culture of hospitality but represent the basic elements that people expect to be in place when they arrive). In the next section we will take a deeper dive into the possibilities for bringing extra attention to these platform level experiences and, by association, the guests who will be made to feel welcome and valued by thoughtful attentiveness to them.

Foundations of Intentional Hospitality

Setting the Stage for Hospitality

Save the best parking spaces available for first-time guests. Post a sign at these spaces. Encourage hospitality team members to notice those parking in these spaces and to provide extra special care to make them welcome.

Have greeters positioned in the parking lot and outside each entry point into the facilities. If it is raining, greeters should have umbrellas available. If people are bringing dishes for a dinner, greeters should be available to help transport dishes.

Have music playing in the background when people enter the worship area. This should be loud enough to overcome the sense of emptiness, but soft enough that it will not interrupt conversations.

Clean and Inviting Facilities

It is common practice for most families to clean up their homes (do the dishes, vacuum the floors, pick up the toys, etc.) when they are expecting guests. We suggest that the same should be true for the family of God as we prepare for guests. The cleanliness of our facilities is a statement about the value we place on guests and the excellence with which we do life together.

The problem is that we who regularly attend worship become so accustomed to things (items collecting in the corner of a hallway, dingy and worn carpets, used bulletins left in the pew racks, peeling paint in the worship center, etc.) that there is a lack of awareness about the way newcomers experience our spaces.

It would be helpful to have someone from outside your church walk the facilities with your trustees to point out areas for improvement.

As a general rule, the cleanliness of facilities and quality of landscaping will not attract people to your church. However, lack of attention to such details might keep them away.

Attractive and Safe Nursery

At the top of the list for most churches is having more young families as part of the congregation. At the top of the list for those young families is having excellent nursery care. It is critical that these facilities are both attractive and safe.

Young moms who carefully select a daycare center for their children will be less than enthusiastic about dropping off the same child to a 15-year-old girl sitting in a rocking chair with several infants crawling around on a dingy area rug.

Are the facilities clean? Are they well-stocked with toys that are sanitized regularly? Is there some form of training/certification required for nursery workers? Is there an identification system with care instructions for each child? Is there a system for contacting parents in worship should the need arise? Is the nursery located in close proximity to the worship space?

Welcome and Hospitality Center

Every worshiping congregation should have a welcome and hospitality center. This is a clearly identified space where knowledgeable guides are present to help newcomers find their way around the campus, escort parents and children to the appropriate classrooms, and help people locate the restrooms.

The welcome center is also a centralized place where guests can get printed information about the ministries of the congregation. Some congregations use this center as the distribution point for gifts prepared for guests in worship.

I believe that this space should also provide a place for people to connect and begin the process of building relationships. Having coffee, juice, and healthy snacks is a good start. Having people from the congregation who invite newcomers to join them for refreshments is even better.

It is often a surprise to congregations that having refreshments located in the fellowship hall or a classroom doesn't seem to be very effective in reaching guests. If this really is a hospitality center, it needs to be clearly visible, central, and identified, so that people unfamiliar with the campus will make this point of contact.

This space is all about relationship building, which is the purpose of hospitality.

Training the Congregation

The importance of having people from the congregation connect with guests and start the process of building relationships cannot be overemphasized. This, unfortunately, is not the natural way for people to do church. They have to be trained. The Rethink Church materials mentioned previously make a couple of excellent suggestions for this training:

- **3-minute rule**: For three minutes following the close of the worship service, ask regular participants to make a point of engaging in conversation with guests and people they do not know rather than rushing out or focusing only on their friends. It takes about three minutes for a guest to exit following the worship experience, and this provides a forum for engaging them relationally.

- **10-foot rule:** Ask all worship participants to make a point of entering into conversation with everyone within a 10-foot radius of where they are sitting at some point prior to or following worship.[9]

- **5-10-link rule:** This rule from Jim Ozier expands the first two rules and adds a third component. Those engaged in conversation with newcomers should introduce them (link them) to someone else with whom they might develop a connection.[10]

Encourage the conversations to focus on getting to know what the guest is seeking and how the church might be helpful. Help guests to connect with others from the congregation, particularly the pastor or staff member who might be of assistance to help them make a connection. Gathering at a hospitality center around refreshments is a good way to facilitate this.

Greetings During Worship

Recent studies have indicated that guests in worship prefer not to be asked to stand and identify themselves (or sit while everyone else stands!). They would rather have some anonymity, or at least they would like to be given permission to make their own choice to put themselves out there. This is particularly true of those younger than retirement age.

Having said that, there are exceptions to the rule. For those congregations with a large demographic of seasonal participants, it is often widely accepted to share who you are and where you are from. This provides a natural connection between the guests and regular participants from the same area of the country and often initiates the building of relationships.

The most effective greeting for guests is not from leaders up on a platform, but from regular people sitting close by who make a point of initiating a conversation. These connections can then be used to get guests to a welcome center where they can find information about the church or be "mugged" (given a gift of a church mug or other small token).

Informational Meetings

I recommend that every congregation have regular (monthly at least) informational meetings where guests can learn about the focus of that particular church, opportunities to grow as disciples, and opportunities to engage the local community. This is a great time to get to know the heart of the pastor and the congregation.

Not every church will be a good fit for every person. The informational meetings provide an opportunity for guests to figure out if this is the right place for them. It is also a natural way to continue building relationships.

Please note, however, that this informational meeting is not intended to be a new member class. It is not the place to review the history of the denomination or local church. It's all about initial connections.

Professional Quality Communications

A consideration too often overlooked as impacting hospitality is the quality of our communications. The website for a church is often the first place that people go to begin forming an impression of your congregation. Is the website attractive? Easily negotiated? Current? Helpful?

Is the outside and inside signage for your facilities adequate to assist people in finding classrooms? Worship center? Restrooms? Will people be turned off by negative signage ("Don't do this!" "Don't enter here!" "Don't walk here!")?

Are your bulletins and newsletters attractive with plenty of white space, illustrations, and of course, useful information presented with good grammar and spelling?

If a PowerPoint is used in worship, is it attractive, checked for grammar and spelling, and not overloaded with too much content? Is there an operator who is trained and experienced to make sure that slides and videos are in place on cue?

Guest Follow-Up

To reiterate the earlier discussion on this topic in this chapter (because it is that important), a critical part of hospitality is the follow-up done with guests who have attended your worship services. At minimum, there should be a letter from the pastor (handwritten is best) welcoming them and expressing appreciation for their participation. A more personal call from someone in the congregation is a plus.

Some congregations provide a brief visit (not necessarily even going into the home) to deliver fresh-baked goods or jellies (preferably made by someone in the congregation) and share a welcome. This provides a personal connection without being overwhelming.

Questions for Leaders and Coaches
Related to Intentional Hospitality

How does this congregation recognize guests?

What form of hospitality center does this congregation offer? Is there a place for people to gather and make connections? Are refreshments offered to facilitate this process? How is sensitivity to families with children demonstrated in the welcoming process?

How does this congregation encourage regular participants to engage guests? What form of training is provided? How is this monitored?

What is the demographic mix of the congregation? How does this compare to the demographics of the surrounding community?

What is the process for following up with first-time guests? What is the role of the pastor?

What is the system for connecting regular participants with first-time guests to help them learn about congregational opportunities?

Does this congregation offer an informational meeting to connect with guests? Who has responsibility for this?

What is the state of the congregation's facilities? Are they clean and inviting—especially the nursery and restrooms?

Is there adequate signage to assist newcomers?

Describe the quality and variety of communication tools utilized by this congregation. Are they up-to-date? User-friendly? Do they avoid the use of "insider" and "churchy" language?

Invitational Hospitality

Refers to the connections made by
the congregation with people they don't
know who are out in the community.

Guiding Principle

**The vast majority of people who visit a church come because
someone invited them. People discover God's love in and
through a relationship with a disciple of Jesus Christ.**

It is no secret that most mainline congregations are aging, in decline, and not drawing new prospects to replace the members they are losing. One of the ways this process can be reversed is through invitational hospitality.

A common rule of thumb is that for a congregation to grow, there needs to be as many yearly guests as there are average weekly participants in worship. Don't miss the importance of these guests: they represent 100% of the congregation's opportunity for new members! Without guests there are no new members. It's as simple as that.

This is a problem, since, as Bob Farr, Kay Kotan, and Doug Anderson point out in *Get Their Name,* the average United Methodist member, statistically speaking, invites someone to church once every 38 years. Some of us are behind schedule![11]

It is also important that we help people distinguish between a "wish" and an "invitation." A wish is where we say something like, "I think you would really like our new pastor. It would be really great for you to come visit someday." An invitation goes more like this:

- "Our church is starting a new message series on _____
  and I was thinking you might find it really helpful."

- "Would you like to come to worship with me this week? I will be glad to pick you up and we could go together."[12]

So how does invitational hospitality work? There are two tracks. First is the track of personal invitations. This is all about current participants inviting their families, friends, neighbors, and acquaintances to come to church. This may seem easier than it actually is for most congregations. There are a variety of reasons for this difficulty. For example, as Claudia Lavy and Dan Glover wrote in *Deepening Your Effectiveness* several years ago, one of the factors influencing whether members of your congregation will invite their friends to worship is their confidence that it would be a good experience (e.g. that worship would be done with a level of excellence).

> The acid test of an effective worship experience is whether or not your average attendee will stake his or her personal reputation among unchurched friends and family on the quality of your worship experience and actually invite them.[13]

That is certainly still a factor, but it is not the only one.

A second factor is that people are just not comfortable making that level of ask. Jim Ozier and Fiona Haworth, in *Clip In*, suggest that rather than asking people to start with an invitation, we should suggest that they start with a recommendation. An invitation requires a higher level of maturity and commitment. On the other hand, mentioning, witnessing, and actively promoting the ministries of the church are things people can do even when they are new to the faith and the church.[14]

A third factor at play is that the church has not done well at helping people understand that part of being a maturing disciple of Jesus is our calling to help people discover God's love and longing for a relationship with them. Jesus put it pretty clearly when he gave the Great Commission to his disciples: "As you go wherever you are going and doing whatever you are doing, make disciples of all people groups, teaching them and baptizing them. . ." (Phil's version of Matthew 28:19).

The second track of invitational hospitality is the connection-building activities of the local church. These connections usually take one of several forms.

Personal Connections

The church has a role in supporting the regular attenders in inviting their friends, relatives, work associates, and neighbors. Some churches provide members with business cards that include the worship times and directions to the church. Many churches provide postcards with information about a new sermon series or seasonal focus that regular attenders can use to invite friends.

Doug Anderson, in his book, *The Race to Reach Out,* shares a seasonal focus approach used by Joe Harding:

- A few weeks before the invitational focus of the season, 3x5 cards are distributed to the congregation.

- Each participant is asked to write down the names of five people they would like to see come to worship.

- Participants are encouraged to take the cards home and display them in a prominent place where they will be reminded to pray daily for the people named on the cards.

- A couple of weeks prior to the invitational focus event, participants are encouraged to extend an invitation.

- In worship the participants are asked, by a show of hands, to be accountable for praying for the people who will be their focus and then making the invitation.

The result was an increase of 50% on these invitational Sundays and a congregation that experienced significant long-term growth.[15]

Networking

This refers to the intentional building of relationships by the pastor and key lay leadership with those out in the community. I have seen over and over again the importance of these relationships forged with community leaders (mayors, police chiefs, fire chiefs, homeowner association officials, school principals, local business owners, and social service organizations). I also recommend that pastors participate in the local Chamber of Commerce and organizations like Kiwanis and Rotary as ways to make connections.

This is important on three fronts: (1) The relationships forged will provide valuable insights into the workings of the community, (2) These relationships will provide further connections in the community, and (3) These relationships model for the congregation the kind of witness that each disciple can provide in their own circle of influence. Another benefit to these kinds of relationships is that through them the congregation will understand their own reputation within the community, which is important to know for future relationship-building and ministry opportunities.

A pastor I coach in the Northeast, following one of our coaching conversations, began to network and have discussions with some people he knew of who were influencers in the community. Not all were immediately receptive, but a conversation with one of them yielded so many additional contacts that the pastor was having trouble getting to all of them. This pastor has begun to encourage his core leadership to follow a similar pattern, and amazing connections are being made throughout the community.

Attractional Ministries

This refers to the types of events that serve to 'attract' people to a congregation through providing visibility and interactions with the local community. Oftentimes these are identified as 'outreach,' but I believe this is a misnomer, since most of them are done on church properties.

These events include things like Fall Festivals, Trunk 'R' Treats (a Halloween gathering in the parking lot with candy distributed from decorated car trunks), Vacation Bible School, pumpkin patches, Christmas tree sales, block parties, concerts, yard sales, and the like. Sometimes these events get a bad rap and are discouraged. I don't feel like there is anything wrong with them—just that they are not a substitute for actually going out into the community. It's a 'both/and' deal. The real value of any of these events (other than raising money) is that they are an opportunity for the building of relationships. By this I do not mean handing out church brochures. If the church is going to host an attractional event, there should be significant thought given to how the event could build contacts for the congregation (providing names and addresses) and how the regular attenders will be encouraged to engage those who come from the community.

A word of caution is in order here. It is often the case that congregations get worn out and distracted doing event after event. The result is that they don't have the time or energy to go farther afield into the community and make a difference. I recommend that such activities be very limited (1–2 per year) to make space for more ministry of engagement.

My colleague Kim Shockley (a ministry coach and wife of a church planter/pastor) learned as part of a church planting team that it was essential to do these types of attractional ministries so that they could make the church name more visible in the community. One of the best opportunities was when they partnered with some stores during the late Christmas shopping season, setting up free gift-wrapping to assist shoppers with packages immediately after purchase. They had plenty of time to chat with the customers during the wrapping process and also invited them to attend the Christmas Eve services. Notice that this congregation moved away from the church grounds to do these attractional events.

Servant Evangelism

This concept was made popular by Steve Sjogren of the Vineyard Church. The basic model is that regular attenders of the congregation engage the local community through service projects. Steve describes servant evangelism as winning the heart before confronting the mind. In a great article, "94 Community Servant Evangelism Ideas for Your Church," he identifies some simple projects any congregation can engage:

- Coffee Giveaways
- Bottled Water Giveaways
- Popcorn Giveaways
- Umbrella Escorts
- Trash Pick-Up
- Shoe Shines
- Surf Wax for surfers at the beach
- Clean Up at Food Courts
- Leaf Raking
- Tree Limb Trimming.[16]

The opportunities for servant evangelism abound. It is an effective witness to God's love. One of the most effective servant activities Kim's church experienced was taking boxes of donuts to fire stations, nursing homes, and other businesses where people had to work on Christmas Eve. The folks took the boxes with them to drop off on their way home from the worship services.

Ministries of Engagement

Often overlooked in the realm of hospitality is the impact of really making a difference in the community and inviting people to engage with the church. This is particularly true for our young adults who frequently enter into a relationship with the church through service.

Ministries of engagement will be discussed further in the chapter on service. For now, let's just say that they are long-term, sacrificial, and needs-focused acts of service to the community. Sometimes the people being served by these impactful ministries will be drawn to the congregational life. Sometimes people with a heart for making a difference will be drawn to the service being offered and then to the community offering it. Sometimes both will happen.

Marketing

This is discussed last because it is the least effective of all the invitational hospitality concepts presented here. Typical approaches include newspaper advertisements, telephone book advertisements, direct mailing, telephone soliciting, and electronic media, including the website.

As a general rule, newspaper and telephone book advertisements are relatively ineffective. Direct mail yields results in the range of one response for every 200 mailers or about ½ of 1% and is fairly expensive. Telephone soliciting is usually seen as an annoyance today.

The website of the church is today's equivalent of an advertisement in the business section of the telephone book a decade or two ago. It is a "must do" and "must do well." Websites must be easy to navigate: invitational and full of pictures, stories, and white space.

Current research indicates that as many as 90% of people will visit a church's website before making a decision to attend. That's huge! If the website is going to be such a primary tool for extending hospitality, it is important that the site represent you well:

- Invest the resources to create a professional-looking site. The quality of your website is considered a reflection of the excellence with which you do ministry.

- Keep the website current. I worked with a church a couple of years ago that had a pastor's message from the previous pastor who had moved two years earlier.

- Have worship times clearly identified with a description of the style of worship included.

- Provide clear directions to your church location. Many websites now include a link to Google Maps or another mapping service.

- Provide information about childcare. Without this, you may lose young families.

- Include information about your staff. The best sites even include a personal statement from staff members.

- Include a place to listen to current messages from worship services.

- Share stories about lives that are changed and the difference the church is making in the community.

Many sites I have visited include an itinerary for newcomers. Information is provided about attire for the service selected, availability and location of childcare, and a time frame for activities the newcomer can experience.

Social Media

It is not uncommon for even our blue-haired worship attendees to be connected to the modern world through Facebook, Instagram, and Twitter with hundreds of friends and followers. This is how we keep up with what is happening in the lives of those we care about.

So, what if the church could leverage those connections?

Imagine the people from your congregation, whether 50 or in the hundreds, each sharing with their hundreds of friends or followers something they are excited about that is happening at the church or even just an invitation to join them in worship. Many churches are preparing jpeg graphics that can be posted along with a personal invitation.

We often treat technology in the church as if it were a distraction rather than a valuable resource. A common experience in the worship of local congregations is the announcement or PowerPoint slide that respectfully requests that you turn off your smartphones in consideration of others.

But what if?

What if we . . .

- Invited worship participants to take out their smartphones as a corporate prayer time is entered and invited them to text someone in need of God's blessing to let them know that they are being prayed for at church?

- Asked those in worship to send a link to their friends inviting them to join the congregation in worship through a live-streamed experience?

- Provided "tweets" that participants could enter on their twitter feeds, highlighting some especially salient point from the message?

- Invited worship participants to text their prayer requests or questions that arise from the message?

These, of course, are just the tip of the iceberg for ways technology could be used as an invitational tool.

Questions for Leaders and Coaches Related to Invitational Hospitality

What kind of networking (building of relationships) takes place by the leadership of this congregation out in the community?

What types of activities are provided to engage the community and promote visibility?

What types of services are offered through the church to support the needs of those living in the community?

How is this congregation involved in direct service to the community?

How are regular participants in the congregation equipped to share their faith and engage those beyond the church?

How does this congregation support community events?

How does the congregation see participation in the life of the community as a ministry of the congregation?

What types of marketing tools are employed by this congregation?

How does the church website reflect a posture of hospitality?

Incarnational Hospitality

Refers to the personal engagement by regular
participants in the congregation in building
relationships with those we know outside the church
in order to be Christ to the unchurched.

Guiding Principle

**People come to a relationship with Jesus through
a relationship with disciples who serve as the
presence of Christ in their lives.**

I hope this doesn't come as a surprise to you.

Some people (perhaps most people) are drawn to a relationship with Jesus through the witness of our lives—how we treat others, the honest way we do business, the priorities we live by, and the giving of ourselves to others. They may seek to get to know us in order to discover how those dimensions of our lives have been developed.

More commonly, we are the ones building relationships with those outside the church with the aspiration of being Christ in their lives. The scope of possibilities for this is almost endless. One new church pastor I know began her congregation by building relationships with young mothers as they had play time at the parks and 'mom time' in each other's homes. The relationships she fostered developed into friendships and ultimately into relationships with Jesus. It is the perfect witness to the Emmaus Walk teaching: "Make a friend, be a friend, bring a friend to Christ."[17]

Christians believe that life finds its meaning in a relationship with Jesus. Since that is true, it becomes the responsibility of every disciple to not only be in that relationship themselves, but to help others discover that relationship as well.

Congregations that do incarnational hospitality well help

their members discover ways to connect with people in times when those people are most open to an expression of God's love for them. For example, people going through major life transitions are often open to support (e.g. marriage, birth of a child, moving to a new community, or a new job). People who are going through crises in life also tend to be open to the loving support offered by disciples (divorce, grief, loss of property, aging, health issues, etc.).

The key to incarnational hospitality is our focus on building relationships beyond the walls of the church. However, in my work around the country with local congregations, my experience has been that focus in this area is not the norm. In fact, just the opposite is generally true. The more deeply people lean in to their church relationships, the more isolated they become from relationships outside the church . . . by a long shot! The more we move within tight circles of church friendships, the less time we have for cultivating non-church acquaintances.

Alan Hirsch, in his book, *The Forgotten Ways,* provides one of the best descriptions I have come across of incarnational hospitality:[18]

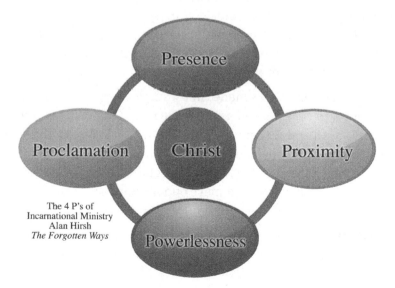

The 4 P's of
Incarnational Ministry
Alan Hirsh
The Forgotten Ways

53

Presence refers to the act of actually being with people. It is what Jesus did when he came into our world. As noted in John 1:14, "The Word became flesh and blood, and moved into the neighborhood" *(The Message)*. Henri Nouwen, in his focus on hospitality, notes:

> It is a privilege to have the time to practice this simple ministry of presence. Still, it is not as simple as it seems . . . I wonder more and more if the first thing shouldn't be to know people by name, to eat and drink with them, to listen to their stories and tell your own, and to let them know . . . that you do not simply like them—but truly love them.[19]

Proximity refers to becoming meaningfully involved in the lives of those being served. There is a significant shift that takes place between the ideas of presence and proximity. In the former, we are close and involved enough to be in a casual relationship. In the latter, we are engaged in ways that make a difference in people's lives.

For example, in the second congregation I served, we offered a meal each week for the homeless, lonely, and hungry in the community. At first, the focus was on getting people (including leadership) involved in preparing, serving, setting up, and cleaning up. We greeted people and got to know many by name. We were practicing the ministry of presence.

Later, a decision was made that we in leadership would not be involved in cooking and serving the meal. Instead, we would actually eat the meal that was being served and sit with the people the meal was designed to be in ministry to. This immediately opened the door to significant relationships, a deeper understanding of needs, and more opportunities to be in service. That was a ministry of proximity.

Powerlessness refers to the understanding that we are servants. Way too often we approach our ministries from a position of power ("fix," "help," "change"). The powerlessness dimension of incarnational hospitality focuses on the servant nature of Christ, working through us to empower others.

Proclamation, of course, refers to the ability and willingness to share the gospel message. As Peter puts it: "Always be prepared to give an answer to everyone who asks you to give the reason for the hope that you have. But do this with gentleness and respect" (1 Peter 3:15).

Proclamation comes last for a reason.

People are most open to the gospel message when we have built a relationship with them, when they know we care about them, and when they understand that we are most concerned with empowering them rather than having power over them. Then we can share, with integrity, the Good News of Jesus Christ.

Since we also understand that people are encouraged in their faith journeys as they are nurtured in Christian community, these relationships formed outside of the church become the bridge to engaging people in the larger community of faith.

It's no secret. Most churches (somewhere around 80%) are plateaued or in decline when it comes to participation in worship. Leadership teams all across the country sit and bemoan the fact that fewer people—and certainly fewer younger people and fewer non-Christian people—are coming to church. They often ask, "What can we do to turn this around?"

My first question is, "Who have you invited to come to church with you in the last month?" For some reason, leadership teams are often surprised by the question. It never occurs to them that this is an ongoing responsibility of *every disciple.* Current research indicates that for those who are unchurched, somewhere between 60–80% responded that they would come to church if someone invited them.

The second question I ask is, "Who are you building a relationship with? For whom are you being Christ in their life so that you might have the opportunity to share God's love for them?" Invitations are less likely to receive a positive response if offered in a vacuum. They are like cold-call sales solicitations. You know the ones we're talking about. The guy selling the amazing solution that will remove any stain from your carpet, the teenager enlisted to get you to subscribe to magazines, or the missionary who wants to share about their *Watchtower* tract. Nobody (okay, almost nobody) enjoys a cold call.

Since it is true that most people come to faith through relationships, how does the church help these relationships happen? I have worked with a surprising number of churches recently that have expressed a need to help their members and friends learn the mechanics of building relationships. This is, of course, a foundational practice in the church for many critical reasons:

- First-time guests are much more likely to feel welcome if worship participants engage them in conversation and take the initial steps to build a relationship.

- Making disciples most often begins with a conversation leading to a relationship, and then leading to a decision to begin the journey of discipleship.

- Members becoming engaged in the life and ministry of the congregation begin this connection through conversations, the building of strong relationships, and developing friendships.

- Those persons engaged through congregational service projects are much more likely to discover the love of Jesus, as these people with natural servants' hearts enter into conversations and develop relationships.

This practice of having conversations and building relationships is a big deal!

How do we develop a skill set for naturally promoting these kinds of exchanges? To build a framework to help congregations make meaningful connections and build relationships that matter:

- First, we must ***catch each other's attention.*** This may take the form of mentioning a family's children or something they're wearing (a sports team logo, flashy tie, or seasonal print), using the proximity of location as an in-road to begin a conversation or just mentioning that you don't know them even though they are sitting next to you.

- Once we have gotten each other's attention, we need to ***establish an interest*** in having a conversation. The obvious interest for those already worshiping together would be their tenure at the church or involvement in church activities. In the case of first-time guests, ask about their experience or how they came to try this church. This movement of establishing an interest could include conversation about families, schools, sports, hobbies, or even favorite restaurants.

- There usually follows a ***period of exploration,*** of asking and answering each other's questions, of probing for areas of common interest, of testing whether they have anything to contribute to us, and whether we have anything to contribute to them. The key here is learning to ask good questions. Be curious! One way we explore our identities is sharing our stories. We grow up, we encounter challenges, large and small, and we figure out how to move forward. The ways we figure out our next moves at these critical junctures reveal the values and interests that really count with us. One of the most direct forms of conversational exploration is to learn each other's stories, focusing on decision points (moments when we are forced to make choices). Why did you go to school here rather than there? Why did you study this rather than that? Why did you decide to emigrate rather than remain at home? As we begin learning each other's answers to these questions, we learn more about each other, what moves us, and what we have to contribute.

- As a result of our exploration, we may begin to ***make exchanges,*** not just in the future, but then and there within the conversation. We may turn out to be a good listener for someone who needs listening. We may find we are learning a great deal from our interaction with the other person. We may find we have an opportunity to offer another person some insight, support, or recognition that they find valuable. We may find we can challenge the other person in ways that may bring them new insight. We may also discover a basis for future exchanges—such as going to see a movie we both want to check out, deciding to go to an event or activity together, or simply taking the next step to have another conversation.

- Finally, if we've determined a basis may exist for a relationship, we *make a commitment* to that relationship by agreeing to meet again, have coffee, come to the meeting, send emails, etc. What turns the exchange into a relationship is the commitment we make to each other and to the future of the relationship. People often make the mistake of trying to skip right to the commitment part without laying a relational foundation first.

Your congregation may find it helpful to do some relationship-building training.

In consultation/coaching work with churches, I often use a tool called the Real Discipleship Survey (available at www. emc3coaching.com). One of the characteristics measured in this survey is the level of congregational maturity in the area of hospitality, specifically the practice of incarnational hospitality. For the vast majority of churches, the composite percentage score for this dimension of hospitality is under 5%. This means that fewer than 5% of the congregation is building relationships outside of the church in order to share God's love with others.

This is a serious issue. If people are not building relationships outside of the church, we are not fulfilling our calling as disciples of Jesus Christ to "go and make disciples." Incarnational hospitality is part of what it means to be a disciple of Jesus. Apparently, we (the church) are not doing so well in helping people to understand this, but there are strategies to promote awareness and facilitate change:

- Preach about incarnational hospitality and invitational hospitality. They are themes easily supported by Scripture, with lots of wonderful examples.
- Teach people in your small groups, leadership teams, committees, circles, and mission teams how to share their personal stories and their faith. As Peter says, "Always be prepared to give an answer to everyone who asks you to give

the reason for the hope you have" (I Peter 3:15).

- Help the members of your congregation to develop a personal testimony.

- Invite people to pray for those who have not yet discovered the fullness of God's love for them.

- Cast a vision for reaching out to people beyond the walls of the church. This is the reason the church exists.

In the United Methodist Church, the membership vows include supporting the church by our *witness.* In the local church, I think we need to be more clear about what this word, witness, means. We need to set some clear expectations, perhaps goals like these:

- Building relationships with at least three people each year to be the presence of Christ in their lives, witnessing the love of God to them.

- Inviting at least three people each year to an event at the church or to a worship experience.

These expectations might be communicated through a membership covenant as described in the "Membership to Discipleship" chapter later in this book.

Churches often encourage participants to "join us for this great mission trip" (to the Bahamas, Haiti, Honduras, Jamaica or even Africa). I wonder what impact we might make if we put the same level of energy into encouraging people to be missionaries in their own neighborhoods.

The cold reality is that most people don't even know their neighbors. They don't know anything about the people who live, literally, down the road. I think this is tragic. After all, Jesus did say something about "love your neighbor." I think he might actually have meant that.

Imagine church members who:

- Intentionally welcome newcomers to the neighborhood

- Host neighborhood gatherings

59

- Adopt a lonely person

- Provide a house watching service for those who are away

- Take care of neighbors' pets.

You get the idea. The possibilities are endless, and the impact can be eternal.

Imagine a church that provides practical support for having their members get to know their neighbors:

- By providing resources for members to use in hosting neighborhood gatherings. One church I encountered had a "party trailer" that had grills, charcoal, paper goods, and utensils. It even had inflatable bounce houses for kids.

- By encouraging members to host Backyard Bible Clubs in the neighborhood rather than just offering Sunday school.

- By holding Vacation Bible School at a park in the neighborhood rather than at the church.

- By supporting small group gatherings in members' homes rather than at the church, making it easier to invite neighbors.

Finally, let's talk about what I call "connecting points." These are what the Celtic people called "thin places." These are times and circumstances in people's lives during which they are more open to the loving support of the body of Christ. These are the times when normal barriers recede, and people long for connection with someone who cares. Deep down, most followers of Jesus get this natural receptivity based on life events, but it might be helpful if the church equipped members to intentionally reach out on these notable occasions:

- Marriage

- Birth of a child

- Move to a new neighborhood

- Divorce

- Loss of a loved one

- Aging

- Health issues

- Loss of property

- Loss of a job.

There are many more thin places and connecting points, of course. Each of them is an opportunity for the body of Christ to provide support, be an expression of God's love, and make lasting connections.

These are also all situations for which the local church could provide support groups.

Questions for Leaders and Coaches Related to Incarnational Hospitality

How are people encouraged and supported in the building of relationships beyond the church?

How are these relationships recognized and celebrated by the pastor and/or congregation?

What types of personal acts of service/mission are being performed by regular participants of this congregation?

How does this congregation use the connecting points of servant evangelism, needs-based evangelism, and ministries of engagement to build relationships in the community and invite participation in congregational life?

Diagnosing the Level of Hospitality

In addition to the questions related to the individual dimensions of hospitality that have been provided for leaders and coaches, there are specific diagnostic tools that you may find helpful:

- **Professions of Faith:** The goal of hospitality is to pave the way for those outside of the church to discover the love of God through a relationship with Jesus Christ. A standard measure of the effectiveness of our hospitality is the trend of the congregation in the area of professions of faith. This information is readily available in most congregations.

- **Communication Tools:** The website, church newsletters, bulletins, and other printed materials utilized by the congregation can provide great insight into the culture of hospitality for a congregation. For example, the website is often the first venue of hospitality experienced by those seeking a church. Does the church have a website? Is it easily navigated? Is it current? Is there information about locating the church and service times and attire? Or, consider the bulletin. One church I worked with had a big negative statement about the use of cell phones in worship right at the top of the worship bulletin. That's probably not the first thing you want people to see! In general, churches should avoid negative signage in any form (e.g., "Keep off the grass," "No drinks in the Sanctuary," etc.). Churches also use a lot of 'churchy' language with the expectation that everyone knows what it means. If you are going to use the Gloria Patri, print or project the text! If you are going to use the Lord's Prayer, print or project the version you use so there is no confusion about 'trespasses' or 'debts.'

- **Readiness 360:** This unique online survey (www.readiness360.com) measures the spiritual intensity, missional alignment, dynamic relationships, and cultural openness of your congregation. Designed to serve as an indicator for readiness to multiply, this is a great resource for measuring church health.[20]

- **Mystery Guests:** It is easy and inexpensive to have someone from outside the church visit the normal worship experience and then report on how they were welcomed and engaged. Excellence in Ministry Coaching has a simple report form you can use that is available at no cost.[21]

- **Welcoming Congregations Training:** United Methodist Communications provides an assessment and training for becoming certified welcoming congregations.[22]

- **Real Discipleship Survey:** This tool is designed for both individual use and as a congregational survey. It highlights the maturity level of individuals in several areas of the discipleship journey, including hospitality. For congregational use, the survey is taken by a representative group and then averaged in each of the dimensions of discipleship as an indicator of the level of maturity for the congregation as a whole.[23]

- **Congregational Survey:** The measurement of hospitality practices as perceived by the congregation is part of a more comprehensive survey of congregational health. This is included in the resource *Tips, Tools, and Activities for Coaching Church Leaders.*[24]

- **Discovering the Possibilities:** This facilitated congregational workshop reveals a variety of insights into the culture of hospitality extended by a congregation. Evaluation tools include a congregational interview, discussion about missional vital signs, facility review, and the Real Discipleship Survey (more information available through Excellence in Ministry Coaching).[25]

- **Leadership Team Assessment:** This document is included in *Tips, Tools, and Activities for Coaching Church Leaders.* It is a set of questions for local church leadership teams to consider. The practices of hospitality, worship, discipleship, service, and generosity are all included.[26]

Most of these and other tools are available in our companion resource for *Shift* and *Shift 2,* called *Tips, Tools, and Activities for Coaching Church Leaders* (see www.emc3coaching.com).

Suggested Additional Resources on Hospitality

- The Race to *Reach Out: Connecting Newcomers to Christ in a New Century,* Douglas T. Anderson and Michael J. Coyner, Abingdon Press, 2004.

- *Right Here, Right Now: Everyday Mission for Everyday People,* Alan Hirsch and Lance Ford, Baker Books, 2011.

- *Reaching Out:* The Three Movements of the Spiritual Life, Henri J.M. Nouwen, Image Books, 1975.

- *The Inviting Church:* A Study of New Member Assimilation, Roy M. Oswald and Speed B. Leas, Alban Institute, 1987.

- *50 Ways to Build Strength to Welcome New People,* Lewis Center for Church Leadership, www.churchleadership.com.

- *Unbinding the Gospel: Real Life Evangelism,* Martha Grace Reese, Chalice Press, 2008.

- Peacemaker Ministries, www.peacemaker.net.

- *Making Peace: A Guide to Overcoming Church Conflict,* Jim Van Yperen, Moody Publishers, 2002.

- *Catch: A Churchwide Program for Invitational Evangelism,* Debi Nixon with Adam Hamilton, Abingdon Press, 2012.

- United Methodist Welcoming Congregation Training, United Methodist Communications, http://www.umcom.org/learn/welcoming-resources.

- *Authentic Community: Practicing The One Another Commands,* Jim Van Yperen, ChurchSmart Resources, 2008.

- Stephen Ministries, www.stephenministries.org.

- *Get Their Name: Grow Your Church by Building New Relationships,* by Bob Farr, Doug Anderson, and Kay Kotan, Abingdon Press, 2013.

Shift 2

From Worship as an Event
to Worship as a Lifestyle

So here's what I want you to do, God helping you: Take your
everyday, ordinary life—your sleeping, eating, going-to-work,
and walking-around life—and place it before God as an offering.

—The Apostle Paul, Romans 12:1 *(The Message)*

You are and always will be a worshiper. It's what you do. You
can't help it. You can't stop it. You can't live without it. But you
can choose where you invest it. . . . We're created to worship.

—Louie Giglio, *The Air I Breathe*[1]

Worship Survey

The survey for this chapter will help you and your congregation explore the quality of your worship experience. Just having key leaders answer these detailed questions will provide valuable insights, but opening this survey to the entire congregation could be revelatory.

(1=Poor . . . 4=Amazing)

	Passionate Worship	1	2	3	4
1.	I attend worship as often as possible, aiming for a minimum of 3 weekends a month.				
2.	The music in worship inspires and lifts my spirit. It is done with excellence.				
3.	I encounter the presence of God in our regular worship services and am inspired to live more fully in the presence of God.				
4.	Our worship services include active participation of the next generations (young adults, youth, and children).				
5.	Worship services are designed to be attractive and engaging for the next generations.				
6.	The worship messages are practical and relevant to my everyday life and encourage me to take next steps in my discipleship journey.				
7.	The worship design enhances my personal worship practices through the introduction of new disciplines and experiences.				
8.	The focus of worship is not disrupted by lengthy stretches of announcements.				

		1	2	3	4
9.	The lessons of Scripture are often presented in creative ways that engage my spirit.				
10.	I leave every worship experience with a clear sense of something I can do to live more fully as a disciple of Jesus Christ.				
11.	I understand the ways in which my offering is making a difference in the community and people's lives.				
12.	Worship experiences are designed in such a way that my senses (sight, sound, touch, smell) are engaged as well as my mind.				
13.	Worship is led by a team including both lay persons and clergy.				
14.	Each worship experience is based on a theme, and every element of worship is designed to bring new levels of understanding.				
15.	The preacher in our worship service shares the message without notes while walking around.				
16.	I regularly feel engaged by the worship experience rather than part of an audience in worship.				
17.	Every worship experience gives me the opportunity to commit more of my life to Jesus.				
18.	The main points of the worship experience are presented so creatively I recall them even weeks later.				
19.	Guests are greeted warmly in worship yet given permission to remain anonymous if desired.				
20.	At some point in each worship experience, I am engaged physically.				
21.	Persons in the congregation make it a point to engage people they don't know in conversation following worship.				
22.	Each worship experience gives clear next steps in my journey as a disciple.				

		1	2	3	4
23.	The design of the worship service provides opportunities to develop new personal spiritual practices.				
24.	Any announcements made during worship provide an opportunity for me to be engaged in the ministry of the congregation.				
25.	Technical support in the worship experience is done with excellence and creativity.				

A perfect score on this survey would be 100 points.

When using this with your leadership team or congregation, here is how you determine an average score:

Total the points for each individual survey. Add the points from all the individual surveys together. Divide that total number by the number of surveys that were completed. This gives you an average score (out of 100 possible points), providing you with a "grade" for your congregational health in this area. Using a standard academic scale:

$$90+ \quad = \quad A$$
$$80\text{-}89 \quad = \quad B$$
$$70\text{-}79 \quad = \quad C$$
$$60\text{-}69 \quad = \quad D$$

What grade does your worship receive? What did the survey reveal? What is your strongest area? What do you hope for in worship? Write your answers in the space below.

It was Saturday evening in the middle of an amazing spiritual retreat weekend. The community had gathered for worship out in the country in a white, framed church that was at least a century old. In this space, where generations of believers had sung praises, prayed prayers, and shared the Word of God together, the Spirit was palpable. We joined the communion of the saints in worship as we lifted our voices in praise and prayer, reflected on the Scriptures together, shared our stories, recommitted our lives, and celebrated at the table of the Feast.

In preparation for the arrival of participants for worship, we lit our candles in the darkened space and sang praise to God who had been at work in such amazing ways. As we, with glowing faces, processed down the aisles between pews, there was not a dry eye in the room. We were there to celebrate what God had been doing. We were there to witness to our faith. Moreover, we were there to encourage the faith of others.

As we left that holy space, each of us understood that our lives had been altered in some unmistakable way. We were no longer on our own. We were part of something bigger than ourselves. We were passionate participants in the mission of God.

There was really nothing especially unique about the elements of the worship service. They were much the same as most worship services in which I have participated. Still, there was something unique about the experience of this particular worship event. In fact, it was so powerful that in over 25 years of ministry, I have had a passion—a longing if you will—to be part of making this kind of impact on people's lives week after week as they, too, gather for worship.

As I reflected on this experience, I developed insights that have been touchstones in leading weekly worship experiences and engaging believers powerfully for over two decades:

- It wasn't about us. The worship experience was about God and focusing our praise and thanksgiving toward the source of our being.

69

- It wasn't showy. The experience had been carefully planned and was well-conducted, but we were careful to be open to what the Spirit wanted to do.

- It was focused. The preaching/teaching of the Word was practical and focused on putting into practice what God wanted for our lives.

- It was experiential. The participants in worship were engaged in acts of worship rather than spectators in a worship event.

- It was relational. We found a joy in gathering with other believers having a similar focus in life, and we were encouraged as we encouraged others.

I'd like to say that these qualities have been the norm for all the worship I have participated in over the years. However, this has not always been the case.

Let's consider some observations about worship, based on current research and my own experiences with coaching congregations in the transformation process:

- Worship is not just an event. It is a lifestyle. What we do in corporate worship provides the opportunity to equip people to be better worshipers the rest of the week.

- A very small percentage of participants in worship report that they have experienced the presence of God during corporate worship over the past year.

- We are designed to worship. The question is what will be the focus of our worship.

- Worship includes both the offering of our lips (praise) and the sacrifice of our lives (service).

- There is no "right" worship style. What is "right" is that the congregation finds a way to connect with the community they are called to serve. Worship is the centerpiece of a Christian community. The excellence and effectiveness with which we offer worship has significant impact on every other dimension of ministry (discipleship, hospitality, service, and generosity).

- Worship experiences that are the result of team planning and execution tend to be more creative and engaging.

In the institutional church, we have become fixated on numbers and, in particular, the numbers in worship participation. On the one hand, this is not all bad, since this data does give us a way of tracking the effectiveness of our worship design and execution.

On the contrary, though, the true measure of worship effectiveness is not how many people come, but how many people live differently because they came. There are a variety of opportunities in worship to lead towards this desired outcome:

- Worship gives people an opportunity to experience the presence of God.

- Worship provides the opportunity to invite people into the journey of discipleship.

- Worship engages us in a process of personal transformation.

- Worship invites us to clear next steps in our discipleship.

- Worship in the corporate setting trains us for worship as a lifestyle.

- Worship re-members the body of Christ.

A Theology of Worship

Worship is about giving honor and glory to God. At a corporate level, worship is the gathering of the community of faith to praise God, learn the ways of God, and be challenged to take the next steps in our commitment as disciples. At a personal level, worship is about living life in a way that honors God in all that we are and do. There is great value to the corporate worship experience. Yet, at the heart of worship, as songwriter Matt Redman puts it, is a life where every single breath is God's—where it's all about Jesus:

King of endless worth
No one could express

How much You deserve
Though I'm weak and poor
All I have is Yours
Every single breath
I'll bring You more than a song
For a song in itself
Is not what You have required
You search much deeper within
Through the way things appear
You're looking into my heart

I'm coming back to the heart of worship
And it's all about You
It's all about You, Jesus
I'm sorry, Lord, for the thing I've made it
When it's all about You
It's all about You, Jesus.[2]

Great worship prepares worshipers to live this kind of worshipful life. It moves us from worship as an occasional event to worship as a daily lifestyle.

It helps define the answers to these lifestyle decisions:

- How I choose to use my time.

- How I choose to use the resources God has provided.

- The focus I place on loving my spouse and family.

- The way I interact with a difficult person.

- The priority I place on spending time with God.

- My faithfulness in following through on commitments.

- The excellence with which I perform the tasks of my job.

These are practical considerations that are resolved moment by moment as we move through each day. They illustrate the potential shift from celebrating worship as a once-a-week event to practicing worship as a daily lifestyle. The truth is, everything we do and every choice we make is an opportunity to worship God or not.

For example, let's say I had a small windfall and now have some extra cash. I can either use that to purchase the Apple watch I have been lusting over, or I can provide additional support to an orphanage in Honduras. The decision I make is either an opportunity to worship God or not.

Or, I'm walking down the street and I see Joe coming toward me. Anxiety starts to creep in as I think about what a talker Joe is. I'm on my way to a meeting and don't want to be late, and I know if Joe and I get engaged in a conversation, there is no way I will make it on time. How I choose to engage Joe, now just a few steps away, is an opportunity to worship God or not.

These examples, of course, just begin to scratch the surface of this shift from worship as an event to worship as a lifestyle. Corporate worship and worship as a lifestyle go hand in hand. Corporate worship prepares us to worship as a lifestyle, and when we practice worship as a lifestyle, it strengthens the celebration of corporate worship.

———— A Liturgical Flow of Worship ————

If the goal of worship is both to provide an opportunity to be engaged in the presence of God and to equip participants to develop a lifestyle of worship, how might one coach the congregation in this area of its ministry? Since many churches use the traditional liturgical flow of a corporate worship experience, let's start there.

Gathering ➡ Praise & Prayer ➡ Proclamation ➡

Response to the Word ➡ Sending Forth

Gathering

This refers to the coming together of the people of God to engage in prayer, praise, learning the ways of God, and taking next steps in the journey of discipleship. In the gathering, people are either led to greater engagement and anticipation for what is to come, or they are left feeling like outsiders and begin to disengage from the worship service. All of this happens before the preacher begins the message! A couple of quick and easy measurements will help you get a sense of the effectiveness of the 'gathering' in your own context: is there a stagnancy in the worship participation with few new people showing up OR are lots of new people floating through but few sticking around? Either is an indication that something is wrong.

I once served a congregation in a small town surrounded by several retirement communities. A regular worship participant from one of these communities shared how a group from her area had originally become involved in the church. She said, "We sat outside in our car and watched people coming out of worship. When we saw that they were smiling and happy to be there, we knew it was the right place for us!"

Praise and Prayer

In some congregations this is actually considered the 'worship' part of the service, while the proclamation is considered the 'teaching' part. I don't like this distinction. However, the praise and prayer component of the service is the beginning of a focus on the God we have come to worship. It is an opportunity to set the stage for the message to be proclaimed. As such, it is important that the musical selections and the prayers voiced relate to and support the main theme of the worship experience.

Proclamation

The proclamation of the Word is usually considered the reading of the Scripture lesson and the message proclaimed from that lesson. This is certainly the core of proclamation. But there is much more! In the contemporary church, we tend to get stuck on the idea of the centrality of the message proclaimed. In my first appointment, the pulpit stood six feet high, was made of granite and shaped like a double-edged sword, with a two-foot-square area for standing to preach. It was placed in front of the altar and the baptismal font, blocking the view except from each extreme side. There was even a brochure explaining the placement and design of the pulpit, emphasizing the "central-ity of preaching" in the worship experience. You can imagine the reaction when the new senior pastor and I moved the pulpit to the side of the chancel and preached at floor level, walking around!

The proclamation of the Word can be made in a variety of ways. For example, there are several websites that offer short video presentations related to a broad spectrum of themes. A drama team might prepare a three-to-five-minute skit to proclaim or introduce a worship theme. A dramatic reading of the Scriptures might be prepared. There might be some type of interactive activity to have the congregation engage with the theme. The point here is that the worship design team should seek the most effective and creative way possible to help make the point and make it stick.

This may also be a good place to introduce a very important concept. To use the words of Cathy Townley (worship coach and author), "Right now, in many of our churches, worship is not our focus; the worship service is. I learned that worship is our relationship with God. That means worship is our way of life. Worship changes our lives. If our lives don't change . . . we are not worshiping."[3]

I agree. Worship is not about an event. It is about a lifestyle. One of the roles of the worship event is to better prepare the congregation to worship as a lifestyle. This certainly includes the presentation of messages that are relevant to people's lives. It includes giving people an opportunity to respond to what God is speaking into their lives during the worship event.

It also includes the introduction of spiritual disciplines. It came as no surprise when my friend Kim Shockley shared that the *Toward Vitality* research project (a United Methodist denominational initiative) showed a congregation that actively participates in the spiritual disciplines of prayer, meditation, Bible study, and other activities that draw us closer to God is more vital because their corporate relationship with God spills over onto others. As she writes in the final report on the project, describing congregations experiencing transformation: "Worship was a source of discipleship formation. . . . Most churches mentioned the practice of John Wesley's means of grace: works of mercy, worship, Bible study, prayer, and even fasting."[4]

While these very things serve as catalysts for maturity as disciples of Jesus Christ, the vast majority of our congregations simply will not attend a class on prayer or spiritual disciplines. During my pastoral ministry, I regularly offered classes on prayer. Much to my surprise (a little sarcasm here), only about one to two percent of the congregation participated, and they were already the 'prayer warriors' of the congregation!

So, to take advantage of the largest opportunity to help people develop their spiritual lives—the worship service—we began to introduce the practice of spiritual disciplines and methods of prayer into the structure of the worship service. These added a new element of creativity to the worship experience and introduced the congregation to tools that would serve them well as they developed their personal worship journey.

Responses to the Word/Proclamation

Communion

I am a huge proponent of including communion as part of every regular worship experience. In the context of the last local congregation I served, this was our practice in every style of worship we offered. There is something about the action of physically receiving the elements of communion and spending time in prayer at the communion rail that allows God the opportunity to speak into people's lives in that moment.

We also provided prayer partners who were available during the communion time to pray with those seeking intercessory support and those making commitments or recommitments of their lives to living as fully devoted disciples. These prayer partners also provided anointing with oil as a vessel of God's healing grace.

In addition to the regular practice of communion, every worship experience included prayer altars located around the sanctuary. These were simple stations that included a tray with sand and a large candle (already lit). We also provided white birthday-cake-style candles that congregants could light from the candle in the center and place in the tray with sand while they offered a prayer of intercession or petition. It was usually the case that people would be lined up waiting for an opportunity to practice this tactile act of prayer.

There is something very significant about physically engaging people in response to the proclamation of the Word. This is a principle that has been demonstrated repeatedly in my work with congregations in renewal. One of the questions posed to workshop participants in "Discovering the Possibilities" (a self-consultative process) is, "Describe a worship experience with this congregation that had an impact on your life and where you knew you were in the presence of God."

Nearly 100% of the time the answers include these types of experiences:

- Christmas Eve Candlelight worship service
- Ash Wednesday worship service
- Healing worship service
- Baptism and baptismal renewal
- Communion
- Consecration of leaders/mission teams.

What do each of these experiences have in common? They engage people physically in some way.

We would also regularly seek other ways to engage people in response to the message. For example, when speaking about the baptism of Jesus, we followed by offering people the opportunity, as they came for communion, to renew their baptismal vows. When preaching about the woman caught in adultery, each congregant was invited to take a small pebble from a bowl beside the communion rail and carry it in their pocket for the week as a reminder about "casting the first stone." On Thanksgiving we created a "wall of thanksgiving" (our version of the wailing wall) on which people could write prayers of thanksgiving. One Easter, working with a theme of the death of Jesus "bridging the gap" between our sinfulness and God's holiness, we built a bridge that people were invited to walk across on their way to communion.

You get the idea. Creatively engaging people in response to the Word makes for a memorable and powerful experience.

Offering

Oftentimes the offering component of the worship service is treated as dead space to fill with an anthem or other musical offering. It has been my experience that there is a great disconnect between the giving of our tithes and offerings and our ability to see that these gifts are making a kingdom difference. People just don't seem to connect the dots. If they can't see the difference their offerings are making (other than paying the bills, which doesn't seem to get people excited), people are less generous. The offering is a great time to introduce the congregation to the impact of ministries, the witness of transformed lives because of the ministries of the church, and the amazing ways the kingdom work is done globally through the connectional system.

Personal testimonies, video testimonies, and prepared video presentations from www.umcom.org are just a few of the many ways the offering time in the worship experience can be used as a tool to encourage extravagant generosity.[5]

This is also a time to witness that the offering is not just about our money. Celebrate the offerings people are making with their lives and their time to make a difference in the community.

If all this is correct and the offering time in worship is not just a way to collect money to pay the budget, it calls into question a significant trend I am finding in some parts of the country. The offering is treated as something we are embarrassed about or something we downplay as almost unnecessary. Offering receptacles are placed at the back of the worship space and people can make a contribution if they think about it. Sometimes the opportunity to make an offering is not even mentioned in the worship service.

Contrast that with the practice of Ghana Wesley UMC in Westbridge, Virginia. This congregation of first and second-generation immigrant families literally dances down the aisle to present their tithes and offerings at the altar. The liturgist announces the offering with the call to the congregation of "Offering Time," and the congregation responds, "Blessing Time." After this is repeated a couple of times, the music begins, and the dance gets underway. This is a time of blessing—both being blessed and being a blessing to others.

People need to be encouraged and taught to be generous. It is part of our spiritual growth.

Sending Forth

This is far more than just the concluding remarks of the worship event. The sending forth is an opportunity to challenge the congregation to take the next step in the spiritual journey, to do something specific in the following week based on what God has been doing through the worship event, and to proclaim God's blessing and power to live as the people God has called us to be.

Since one of the things we hope to accomplish as we send people forth is the building of relationships and the expression of hospitality, this is also a great opportunity to encourage this practice. An invitation can go something like this: "Our hospitality center is located just outside the worship center, and there are lots of great refreshments for you to enjoy. If you are sitting close to someone you do not know, invite them to join you for a cup of coffee or juice and take an opportunity to begin a new friendship."

This approach takes the pressure off "activating our guest location radar" and guests wondering if someone will choose them (imagine choosing teams in elementary school and the fear that created). Everyone is encouraged to engage someone else in building a relationship.

Questions for Leaders and Coaches Related to a Liturgical Flow of Worship

Who is the target group for the worship experience? How does this form the way worship is designed?

What is the "mood" of the gathered worship community? What are their facial expressions and body language? How do the choir and those leading worship reflect a worshiping attitude?

What is the quality of printed materials distributed for worship?

How is the worship experience designed to reflect a culture of excellence?

How does the leadership of worship include all ages and demographic groups represented in the congregation? Are there ages or groups missing?

What is the musical style most prevalent in your worship experience? Does this reflect the demographics of the congregation? Of the community?

What opportunities exist in your worship for participants to take a next step in their discipleship journey?

How are people invited to explore a relationship with this community of faith?

The liturgical flow described previously is a standard approach to designing worship. It has been used in pretty much the same form for centuries. Yet, when regular churchgoers were surveyed by George Barna, a significant number admitted that they hadn't experienced God's presence in the past year. In other words, the worship didn't connect. As Barna writes, "Our studies show that 14 percent of adult believers admit that they have never experienced the presence of God, 14 percent have experienced His presence but not in the past year, and 72 percent have encountered God in a real way within the past year. In a typical worship service, about half claim that they did not experience God's presence or feel that they interacted with Him in a personal way."[6]

I believe that one of the reasons for the disconnect may be our lack of central theme or message, connecting the individual parts to the whole worship experience. For example, we may sing about the majesty of God, pray for the sick in our midst, hear a message about the lost sheep, and then be sent out to be lights in the world. It's hard to imagine how this disjointed experience would be transforming or inspire us to develop a lifestyle of worship.

Another reason that people may not connect with worship is that we who design it give little consideration to the ways in which people receive, process, and act on the information and experience. A planning tool that I have found helpful (in both worship and curriculum design) is a resource called 4MAT. This tool, created by Dr. Bernice McCarthy, founder of About Learning, Inc., considers the various learning styles (closely associated with the MBTI, for those familiar with this tool) and helps engage all learners when creating a learning experience.[7]

Let's start with how learners learn:

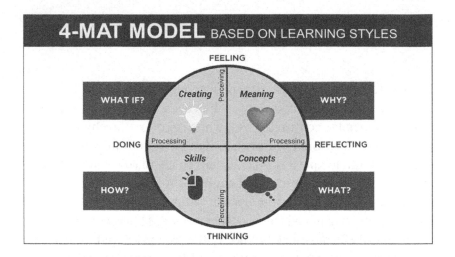

Notice the two axes of this diagram. The vertical axis or line refers to how learners perceive: in other words, how they take in the things they learn. Some people sense or feel things. Others need to think about the things they learn. The horizontal axis or line refers to how learners process or what they do with what they take in. Some people process what they take in by reflecting on it, mulling it over. Others process by doing something with what they take in.

Now let's look at how these differences in perception and process produce different types of learners:

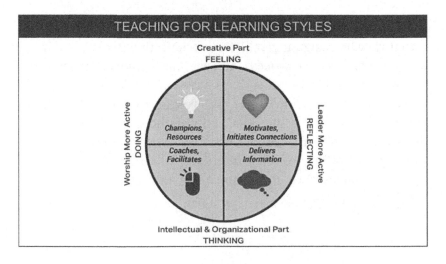

Each learning style can be identified by a question:

- Why?—These worshipers feel and then reflect. They need to know why something is significant and sense it in their hearts before they will engage with it. They might be described as 'heart people' because they need to feel deeply to connect.

- What?—These worshipers think and then reflect. They need information before they can begin to process what is being asked of them. They might be described as 'book people,' because they need content or concepts to connect.

- How?—These worshipers think and then do. Like the "what" people, they need information, but they process by putting what they learn into action. They might be described as 'tool' people, because they need practical content to connect. If these worshipers can't do something with what they have learned, the learning is lost.

- What If?—These worshipers feel and then do. Once they sense something is important, they are already moving to doing and applying what they are taking in to other parts of their lives. They might be described as 'rocket' people, because once they feel deeply, they are ready to take off.

In every worshiping community all four types are represented. If we fail to address any one of the questions, people may leave without engaging with the Word in any significant way.

Let's look at an example of worship designed around the 4MAT Wheel:

For this worship experience, the theme is "Your War Room." We will use the text from Mark 1:35, which reads, "Very early in the morning, while it was still dark, Jesus got up, left the house and went off to a solitary place, where he prayed."

As the congregation gathers for worship, they enter a worship space (sanctuary) that is darkened and filled with candles on tables all around the room. Projected on the screen or scattered around the room are images of war, hungry children, broken families, run down school facilities, etc., with a strong focus on needs represented in your community and concerns of your people.

The opening welcome emphasizes the hope of the people gathered in the midst of a world in need of a Savior to drive out the demons. The opening hymn or praise choruses celebrate the power and presence of a God who has overcome evil and is at work in the world today.

The corporate prayer acknowledges the broken, hurting world around us and the hope of new life (resurrection) through the power of the Holy Spirit and the willing engagement of committed disciples.

The Lord's Prayer is sung as a special musical selection.

Additional hymns or praise songs focus around the power of prayer. Perhaps a reading from the Psalms (the prayer book of the Bible) is included.

The Scripture is read with some context providing the framework of getting time away to focus on God, empowering the next steps of proclaiming the Word.

The offering is received as a means of providing support for a hurting world. A testimony is provided about the difference the church is making in the community.

The message is focused around the power of intercessory prayer and includes a video clip or at least the story line from the movie, *The War Room*. Testimony is provided about lives that have been touched through the power of prayer. Instruction is given about how to have a personal devotional and intercessory prayer focus. Perhaps a witness from the congregation shares about how they personally practice this in daily life. The congregation is invited to write down on five 3x5 cards the names of persons they know need healing and hope, and to commit to pray for these people during the next week.

At the conclusion of the message, the congregation is

invited to receive communion specifically as a means of grace empowering a life of hope. People are invited to a time of prayer at the altar rail after they have received communion. There, prayer partners are available to pray with them and anoint them if desired.

As people are returning to their seats, they have an additional opportunity to pray for someone by lighting a candle at the intercessory prayer altars.

The closing song(s) are uplifting and focused on the God who is gracious and desires to bring abundant life to all.

Closing announcements (limit of three announcements and three minutes total for making all of them) focus on opportunities for the congregation to be involved in making a difference in the community/world.

As the Benediction (or closing prayer) is offered, people are encouraged to use the distributed prayer guide during the upcoming week.

You may have noticed several things about this worship scenario:

- A single clear theme
- An environment that supports the theme
- Clear connections for why, what, how, and what if?
- Every element of worship supports the theme
- Clear next steps for discipleship (living out the message)
- Practical support for next steps
- Participatory elements (engage the body and the mind)
- All liturgical elements are present
- Creative presentation (because people remember what is done creatively).

A church of any size can create this kind of worship experience with a little advance planning. There are plenty of opportunities for members of the congregation to be using their creative gifts (e.g. altar arrangements, prayer altars, prayer partners, technical support if available, music leadership, Scripture reading/introduction, writing/leading corporate prayer, visuals, testimonies, witnesses). Or, this can all be done with a couple of people planning and preparing for worship.

We have long heard it said that people remember less than 10% of what they hear from our worship messages. What people take away from the worship experience is based on more than what is presented in the message. If done well, the whole worship experience is built around a theme, and everything that is done connects to and reinforces that theme. This certainly includes the selection of music that relates to the message. It, of course, means the message is based on the Sripture selected, and helps people take the principles presented in the Word and apply them to their daily lives. It also includes creative ways of presenting the message so that we move beyond the standard lecture and reading methods, interactive elements that encourage the participants to respond to what God is doing in their midst, visual elements (altar arrangements, banners, bulletins, etc.) that reinforce the message, prayers and readings that tie directly into the message, and even the way in which participants greet each other.

For more information about the 4MAT process, go to www. aboutlearning.com. There are lots of great resources to help you get started.

The following list is a sampling of creative design elements that could be used in preparing for and leading worship:

CREATIVE DESIGN ELEMENTS

ASTHETICS

- Banners with theme of message series.
- Creative altar design.
- Backdrops for skits (e.g. historical scenes, bridge).
- Gathering Area/Narthex design.
- Use of children's drawings and paintings in gathering area/worship space.

PRINTED MATERIALS

- Bulletin cover with message theme highlighted.
- QR code in bulletin.
- Newsletter themed with articles related to message series.
- Devotional guides for families related to series.
- Discussion guides for small groups.
- Take-Away reflections and next steps from message.
- Take-Away info for co-workers or neighbors with series info.

SIGNAGE

- Marquee on church sign related to message series.
- Art displayed in entryway/worship center.

MUSICAL SELECTIONS

- All music for worship should reinforce the message theme.
- Worship leader may introduce with story or scripture.
- Intentional focus on congregational music being "sing-able."
- Flash-Mob Choir opportunities for children, youth, and adults.

MEDIA

- Video selections related to theme/illustrating theme – used in message or welcome time.
- Powerpoint slides with image that reinforces the message theme.
- Moving backgrounds or other static imagery reinforcing the message.
- Incorporate children, youth, and adult art through scanning to digital media.
- Website with theme image for series.
- Facebook check-in with announcements or call to worship.
- Encourage tweeting sermon with use of hashtag for worship.
- Encourage prayer texts from worship to friends/family.
- Capturing testimonies and ministry areas on video to allow a "window" into new opportunities and touched lives.

DRAMA/EXPERIENTIAL

- Skits developing message theme.
- Testimonies/witnesses.
- Message.
- Next steps following message.
- Sacraments – tied to theme.
- Prayer teams/healing and anointing – tied to theme.
- Poetry.
- Health kits for UMCOR assembled during the service; praying over lives that will be touched by ministry.

LITURGY

- Scripture selections.
- Prayers that reinforce theme.
- Dramatic readings.
- Psalms.
- Video liturgy.

SUPPLEMENTARY

- Materials, such as recommended books at Welcome Center.

No worship planning person or team is going to use all of these ideas. They are just that—ideas to get the pump primed.

Remember, worship that is done well shares these qualities:

- Central theme
- Creative presentation
- Clear next steps for discipleship
- Engagement of the body as well as the mind.

I want to re-emphasize the value of a themed worship, or what Dave Ferguson calls "The Big Idea." If you want participants to leave worship with a clear understanding of what God wants for them or next steps in discipleship, everything needs to point to that central theme. We often muddy the waters by not paying attention to this central design element.

For example, in the worship scenario described previously:

- The welcome/greeting is focused on the hope we have as a people who believe that God will redeem the brokenness of our world and that our intercessory prayers invite that redemptive activity.
- The announcements focus on opportunities to be engaged in bringing hope and healing to this broken world.
- The songs (hymns or praise songs) focus on the power of prayer.
- The prayer (corporate or pastoral) includes specific needs of the community and world.
- The Scripture selection points to the power of prayer.
- The message invites us to be actively engaged as intercessors for our world through our prayers.
- The offering includes a witness to the difference the church makes in bringing hope and healing to our world.
- The communion invitation highlights our "being one in ministry to the world."

- The next-steps focus is on how the congregation can be involved in intercessory prayer and living a life bringing hope and healing.

- The benediction sends us out to be the ambassadors of Jesus by bringing a message of hope and healing to the world.

All of this takes planning and preparation but results in the difference between routine and impactful worship. Finding a way to do this often means the difference between routine and amazing worship!

Let's consider a second example from a World Communion Sunday worship experience with the overarching theme of Jesus as the Bread of Life.

As people enter the sanctuary/worship center, they immediately notice that something special is happening. Every wall is adorned with flags of nations from around the world. Background music is playing familiar tunes, but the vocals are in unfamiliar languages. The altar table is piled high with breads from several different cultures. Bread machines are positioned in the back of the sanctuary, filling the space with the aroma of fresh baked bread. Participants in worship who come from other countries have been invited to dress in their native garb.

The musical selections are chosen to be sung in both English and another language. (*The United Methodist Hymnal* offers a good variety.)

The prayer is offered in a language other than English, with a translation provided.

The message is focused on the theme of "Changing the World One Life at a Time" and includes a video testimony from a worship experience in another country. If the technology is available, this can even be done in real time.

The offering time includes a testimony about the difference the church is making in the developing world that is possible only because of the generosity of people like those gathered in this space.

As people come for Holy Communion, they are reminded that this sacrament is a foretaste of the heavenly banquet where people from all nations will gather at the feast God has prepared. They are invited to consider their circle of influence, the possibilities for being Christ in people's lives in their community, and their involvement in international missions. They may also choose to try a type of bread from another culture as a symbol of our unity in Christ.

The benediction invites the congregation to offer the Bread of Life to the world around them, crossing the barriers of culture, race, ethnicity, age, and lifestyle. The Bread of Life is available to all and is presented through our faithfulness in life.

Worship does not have to be routine! Imagine the possibilities for your worship experiences as you consider creative ways to engage the congregation. The following worship planning guide may be helpful as you build worship experiences.

WORSHIP PLANNING GUIDE

DATE:	THEME / TITLE:
Scripture Selection	
What's the Point? (one sentence summary)	
How does this message apply to people's lives?	
What's the 'take away'? (what do you want people to do/be?)	
Brief Outline	
Creative Elements for communicating the message	(illustrations, video clips, dramatic readings, skits/drama, etc.)
Creative Elements in Worship Design	(altar arrangements, banners, readings, questions, prayers, supporting materials)
Musical Selections	

Who Are You Trying to Reach with Your Worship?

There are many options for designing creative worship. So, what is the driving factor in selecting the options that will be most effective for you?

Most of the time that driving factor seems to be the preferences of the current worshiping congregation. A church with which I still have strong ties recently completed an extensive survey of the congregation with worship as the main focus. While I applaud the desire of leadership to seek the involvement of the congregation, it soon became clear that the design of the survey provided a forum for people to share their personal preferences. This is typical, even without a formal survey process.

Perhaps it is time for a shift in thinking brought about by the questions we ask. For example, what if we switched from "What do you like or dislike about our current worship experience?" to "What kind of worship experience would we need to provide to reach the people in our surrounding community?"

The starting point in addressing the second and bigger question is to understand the demographics of your community. While there are a variety of ways to get this information, the most helpful and insightful resource I have found is Mission-Insite (missioninsite.org). A simple QuickInsite Report will provide you easily accessible information about Mosaic Groups (Lifestyle Groups) in your community. I typically recommend exploring the needs of the top three groups.

Tom Bandy, in his book *Worship Ways,* provides an in-depth resource for exploring the worship opportunities that engage the various demographic segments which are broken down in a meticulous analysis of the designations known as Mosaic Groups. For example, the Coaching Worship style is preferred by the Mosaic Groups known as "Kids and Cabernet," "Generational Soup," "No Place Like Home," "Fast Track Couples," "Diapers and Debit Cards," "Family Troopers," "Rolling the Dice," "Hope for Tomorrow," and "Small Towns, Shallow Pockets." You can see that this is precisely tuned data analysis. It's a great example of using modern technology to calibrate your ministry approach, and it's a lot of fun to learn these kinds of details about your local community and what makes it click.

The following table, from *Worship Ways,* gives insights into the relationships between the needs of people and the worship styles that are most engaging for specific groups.[8] It is a further illustration of the detailed analysis that you can use to connect worship practices to worship participants. There are many resources available to help you think tactically about how you structure and lead worship.

Worship Options	Addressing Life Situations	Catalyst for Acceptance	Christ Experience	Resolving Existential Anxiety
Coaching Worship	Lost Looking for direction	Life Purpose and Destiny	Spiritual Guide	Emptiness
Educational Worship	Lonely Looking for Rapport	Authentic and Truthful Relationships	Perfect Human	Meaninglessness
Transformational Worship	Trapped Looking for Deliverance	Liberation and Fresh Start	New Being	Fate
Inspirational Worship	Dying Looking for Renewal	Confidence for Enduring Life	Promise Keeper	Death
Healing Worship	Broken Looking for Healing	Wholeness and Serenity	Healer	Guilt
Mission-Connectional Worship	Abused Looking for Vindication	Advocacy and Justice	Vindicator	Shame
Care Giving Worship	Discarded Looking for Compassion	Belonging and Comfort	Shepherd	Displacement

Questions for Leaders and Coaches
Related to Worship That Connects

Who is the target group for the worship experience? How does this form the way worship is designed?

In what ways is the preaching/teaching relevant to the everyday lives of people trying to honor God?

How are images and video included to support the message theme?

How is variety built into the weekly worship experiences to avoid a sense of routine?

How are people given an opportunity to respond to the message? Share some of your most exciting activities.

How much freedom does the pastor have (use) to move away from reading a prepared manuscript?

How are worship themes selected?

How is the proclamation of the Word supported by elements of worship beyond the preaching/teaching?

How is the theme of worship developed as the congregation prepares for the worship experience or follows up on the worship experience?

What opportunities exist in your worship for participants to take a next step in their discipleship journey?

Worship Design Teams

I remember clearly the days when I handed my secretary a form that indicated the hymns selected, Scripture reading, message title, and responsive readings, so that she could put together the bulletin for Sunday morning. That concluded my "worship planning" for the week (except for writing the message of course)!

That was then, but in the new post-Christian age, churches that are growing commonly share the following worship planning practices:

- Spend significant time in planning for worship, long term and weekly
- Prepare extensively for each worship experience
- Regularly evaluate and revise what they are doing
- Pay attention to how worship impacts every dimension of discipleship.

Worship design for me, and for pastors who are experiencing the amazing power of creative worship design, has come a long way. Most of that is due to the realization that we provide a much more creative, impactful, and engaging worship experience when a carefully selected team prepares it.

In my setting, the team included my assistant to the pastor (also a creative writing instructor and amazingly creative individual), my youth director (a great presenter in his own right and very creative thinker), a member of the praise team (especially aware of the resources in the music world), myself (a not-so-creative thinker but good organizer and worship leader/presenter). This core group was supplemented by a technical support team, a visual design team (altar arrangements and banners), a drama team, and other music leaders, all of whom participated in worship planning based on availability and need. The full team also met once a month.

Drawing on the work of Len Wilson and Jason Moore in *Taking Flight with Creativity: Worship Design Teams That Work*, I would certainly include on this team a new believer if I were leading a team today. This would keep me from using language that is too churchy or concepts that are not understood by those beginning the faith journey.[9]

The creativity in the worship experience (both the traditional service and more modern praise service) was a huge factor in the growth of that congregation over our years together. Still, it wasn't without effort and risk.

To be honest, we lost a few people when the church leadership decided to install the projection system in the sanctuary. A couple of people said they just couldn't worship where there was a screen (so, I referred them to a church where they would probably never install a screen). Being sensitive to the expectations of the more traditional worship service attendees, we did not use the projection system or most of the creative elements regularly in the traditional services for nearly a year. Eventually, the participants in the traditional services asked for us to include these! The request came something like this, "How come you never do any of the cool stuff in our service that you do in the praise services?" At that point we knew the time was right.

Working with a worship team also takes more time and energy on the part of the pastor. I promise you it is worth it, and you will see the results in the connections made in worship. I suggest planning message series several months in advance (titles, themes, Scriptures, and a brief paragraph indicating the direction the message is planned to take). This planning document is shared with the Creative Worship Team members, who begin to watch for illustrations, movie clips, stories, data, and resources around the themes. These are shared with the pastor in the weekly meetings.

A month out, the pastor provides the team with an outline of the message and proposed illustrations or other creative elements. The team begins to build the creative elements of the worship experience beyond the message.

Two weeks out, the team locks in the basic flow of the worship experience and has communicated special needs for video support (clips or creating a video), drama, visual arts, etc.

A week out, the pastor presents a draft of the message to the team for review. While this was initially a very intimidating experience, it was amazingly helpful. Often the team would suggest a better illustration or help change the language to something less churchy and easier to connect with.

A spreadsheet was prepared for each worship experience with every element identified and timed. The person responsible for leadership of each element was identified and any special instructions for transitions described. During the service, the assistant to the pastor served as the producer, making sure that everyone was ready for his or her role.

Every worship service included what I call the GPS focus:

- **G**od-centered: What God has done, who God is, what God is saying to us, what God is asking us to do or be, and where God is at work in our world.

- **P**articipatory: A focus on engaging people actively in the worship experience, giving them something to do, some way to respond to what God is doing in their midst.

- **S**ensory: Finding ways to engage the senses, not just the brain. We tried to find ways to create visual connections, smells, tastes, and touches that helped people engage the Word.

Questions for Leaders and Coaches
Related to Worship Design Teams

How are the seasons of the church year and special events used to extend special invitations to the community?

What options are you considering for worship as you look to future needs?

What team(s) is/are in place to support the process of gathering for worship? How are they trained?

What is the quality of printed materials distributed for worship? Are the materials designed with the expectation that those unfamiliar with your worship experience could be present?

How are worship themes selected?

How does the design of the worship experience engage the next generation?

Is the preaching/teaching relevant to the everyday lives of people trying to live as Jesus calls them?

What role does a Creative Worship Team play in the development of the message to be presented or in the focus on the Scriptures?

How well does the service demonstrate a GPS focus: God-centered, Participatory, and Sensory?

Using Corporate Worship as Congregational Training for Worship as a Lifestyle

Think for a moment about all the things that are part of your regular worship experience. Name at least 10 of them in the blank space below:

You probably came up with some of the following, and probably some that are not identified:

Prayer, Songs/Hymns, Offering, Message, Greeting, Scripture Reading, Response to the Word, Witness/Testimony, Benediction, Communion, Baptism, Responsive Readings, Altar Call/Time of Prayer, Announcements, Prayer Requests, Recognition of Guests.

These are all good things to do. They are also all ways that we can support worship participants in having a stronger worship lifestyle. There are key areas in which the link between corporate worship experience and the worship lifestyle are strongest:

- **The Message / Sermon:** This is the easiest one. The message is a great opportunity to help people see the relevance of God's Word to their daily lives. We can give practical ways to live the way God intends for us.

- **Prayer:** In all my years of ministry in the local church I offered an annual class on prayer. The problem was that only about one percent of the congregation participated, and those were already our 'prayer warriors'! Where does the rest of the congregation learn how to pray? With over 80% of regular worshipers wanting help in developing a personal relationship with Jesus, how do we help them if they don't come to a prayer class? I would suggest that the worship service gives us a great opportunity. What might be the result if we were to introduce a model of prayer (described in the bulletin, e.g., ACTS, ACTIP, the petitions of the Lord's Prayer) and then explained how that model would be used for the pastoral prayer? At the conclusion, the congregation is then invited to try that prayer model for the next week.

- **Scripture:** Again, research indicates 80% of regular worshipers have a need of learning how to study the Scriptures and apply them to daily life, but only a small percentage attend a Bible study. What if we were to introduce some easy Bible study tools as part of the Scripture presentation in worship? For example, a theological Bible study or reflective Bible study tool.

- **Spiritual Disciplines:** How might the congregation's connection to God be enhanced if we were to use the worship service to introduce them to things like praying the Scriptures, guided meditations, or how to have a daily devotional time?

- **Offering:** What if we, instead of just receiving the offering and providing an anthem, shared actual witnesses about the difference our sharing is making in the lives of those who give and/or those who receive? Sometimes we just need to help people connect the dots.

- **Greeting:** Even the greeting time can be a tool to help people see that hospitality is bigger than just saying, "welcome to church." What if we were to encourage a real conversation and then ask people to continue that conversation following worship at the hospitality center?

The possibilities are endless. So is the difference it can make in the practice of a worship lifestyle.

Engaging in Personal Worship

A personal devotional time is a spiritual practice that deepens our connection to, and relationship with, God. As we develop an awareness of God through the spiritual practices, we also increasingly develop an awareness of God at work in all the moments of our lives.

While all churches seem to expect people to have a personal devotional time, they sometimes are not so clear on how to do that. We want to remedy that. So, let's talk about how to have a personal devotional time.

Pick a time of day that works for you.

- Some people prefer to start the day with a focus on God.
- Others prefer to end the day that way.
- Some people like both.

Pick a place that works for you.

While the movie, *The War Room,* recently made the idea of a prayer closet popular, you don't actually have to set aside a room strictly for this purpose. Having a quiet space with a comfortable chair is a good starting point.

Set aside some time that is just for paying attention to God.

While the timeframe of an hour is often touted as the ideal, we suggest that you start slowly. Five or 10 minutes a day would be a great starting point.

How to spend your time.

- Offer praise to God. Some people find that listening to or singing along with praise songs or hymns is helpful. Others begin by reading a Psalm of praise.

- Engage in a time of prayer. There are a wide variety of models for prayer. You may want to explore several types. My book, *Foundations: An Introduction to Christian Practices,* is a great primer on a variety of prayer models.

- Spend time reflecting on the Scriptures. Reflective reading means that we don't just read through a few verses of Scripture, but that we consider what the Word is asking of us. How might our lives be different if we were to live as the Scriptures suggest?

- Journal. Keep a journal of what God is revealing through your times of devotion and reflection along with prayer requests and answers.

- Pray your calendar. When beginning the day with a devotional time, pray for the people and the activities of the day. When ending the day with a devotional time, reflect back on the day (people and activities) and where you see God at work.

- Thank God for the time together.

Diagnosing the Level of Worship Engagement

- **Mystery Worshipers:** It is easy and inexpensive to have someone from outside the church visit the normal worship experience and then report on how they were welcomed and engaged by the event. Excellence in Ministry Coaching has a simple report form that is available at no cost.[10]

- **Real Discipleship Survey:** This tool is designed for both individual use and as a congregational survey. It highlights the maturity level of individuals in several areas of the discipleship journey, including worship. For congregational use, the survey is taken by a representative group and then averaged in each of the dimensions of discipleship as an indicator of the level of maturity for the congregation as a whole.[11]

- **Congregational Survey:** The measurement of worship practices as perceived by the congregation is part of a more comprehensive survey of congregational health. This is included in the resource, *Tips, Tools, and Activities for Coaching Church Leaders.*[12]

- **Discovering the Possibilities:** This facilitated congregational workshop includes a variety of insights into the culture of worship extended by a congregation. These insights are gathered through congregational interviews, discussion about missional vital signs, facility review, and the Real Discipleship Survey.[13]

- **Leadership Team Assessment:** This document is a set of questions for local church leadership teams to consider. The practices of hospitality, worship, discipleship, service, and generosity are all included. These assessments are included in the resource *Tips, Tools, and Activities for Coaching Church Leaders.*[14]

- **Worship Survey:** This document is a congregational survey providing insight into the experience of worshipers.[15]

Most of these and other tools are available in our companion resource for *Shift* and *Shift 2*, called *Tips, Tools, and Activities for Coaching Church Leaders* (see www.emc3coaching.com).

Steps for Getting Started

In my work with congregations across the country, I have found several practices that are essential to the development of a culture of congregational worship. These do not represent the end-goal of worship. Instead, I have found that these are the foundations upon which a culture of passionate worship is built. (Some of this will be a reformulation of things you have read earlier in the chapter, but they are included here to reinforce their importance as one of several practical steps for moving your ministry forward.)

It Takes a Team

Congregations which consistently provide meaningful, creative, and relevant worship experiences have found that worship planning and execution is better accomplished by a team, often called the Creative Worship Team. This team can include staff members and must include the pastor, but it should also include members of the congregation—be sure to engage a new believer—who bring a level of creativity and perspective to the development process that is stronger than the insights of any one person alone.

The team ought to include representatives from those groups involved in executing worship (e.g., praise team, choir, etc.).

This process of designing worship does require some planning ahead, since the pastor will need to have themes, Scriptures, and even general observations about the direction of the message prepared well in advance.

Plan for GPS Worship

As noted previously, as you plan for worship, we encourage the use of a GPS model—God-centered, participatory, and sensory.

- God-centered: The focus of worship is on what God has done, who God is, what God is saying to us, what God is asking us to do, and where God is at work in our world . . . or would like to be.

- Participatory: Worship is not a spectator sport. People want to be included in what is going on rather than just being passionate observers. How could your worship provide ways for people to participate?

- Sensory: Much of worship tends to be from the eyebrows up, but we are more than just brains. We can touch, taste, see, smell, hear, and feel emotions. What are some ways that your congregation has involved people's senses in worship?

Focus with a Single Unifying Theme

We believe the most powerful worship experiences are usually those that have a single, unifying theme. Life is complex—overwhelmingly so. People are bombarded with message after message all day long, all competing for their attention and none really getting it. The same thing can happen in worship. Consider all the competing messages people receive in any given worship service: several different announcements, songs that each have a message, prayers that communicate yet another message, special opportunities for service or giving, and then the Scripture and message, with lots of random additional elements depending on the needs of a congregation in any given week.

Simple is in. Worship just works better when there is a unifying theme, and everything done in worship helps build that theme. Those who plan worship should be able to tell you the theme for every service, and everything in the service ought to serve that strategic focus.

Reinforce "The Big Idea"

Dave Ferguson, in his previously mentioned book, *The Big Idea* (a great read for worship teams), suggests that this idea of theming should go beyond even the worship event. If you really want people to get the big idea, reinforce it through a church-wide experience. He notes that the typical weekend worshiper is bombarded with nearly 20 different ideas during the worship experience.[16]

Helping the congregation grasp the week's big idea is more likely if you do things like these:

- Develop a study guide based on the theme of worship for use by Sunday School classes and small groups.

- Provide devotional thoughts for the week built around the worship theme.

- Give families the opportunity to share the theme together through family devotions.

• Give practical tips for living out the theme in real life (developing a worshipful lifestyle).

Present Important Truths in Unforgettable Ways

Studies show that people remember less than 10% of what they hear. That's why the unifying theme is so important—the message is presented in a variety of ways.

Use odd images, humor, video clips, witnesses, songs, skits, stories—use whatever you need to help people remember what you really want them to remember.

Make It Relevant

People are looking for practical ways to live out their faith. There is so much in Scripture that needs to be applied to people's everyday lives as they seek to live faithfully under the lordship of Jesus Christ and to join him in service to others.

Too often in worship, there is discussion around word studies and historical facts that have absolutely nothing to do with where people live—no matter how interesting the preacher may find them. For people to sense God speaking to them in worship, they need to sense that what is being communicated has something to do with real life. If it doesn't, why use the gift of their time talking about it? Someone once told me, "Don't give them the recipe—serve the pie!"

Provide Practical Next Steps

People begin to build into their lives the behaviors that will form their attitudes and feelings as they are given solid next steps to take when leaving worship. It is important that worship leaders/preachers help people connect the dots—to see exactly what the message means in real, practical terms. In other words, how does one actually live into this?

What practical steps do people need to be challenged to take in the coming week to live into the theme of your worship?

Minimize Announcements

I know that this can be a touchy subject. The truth is that announcements take over too many worship services. Here are two rules that can prevent this from happening:

- **3 in 3**: This means that there are only three verbal announcements, and that they are made in just three minutes—either before or after the worship experience. Announcements should not be sprinkled throughout the worship service like advertisements in a TV show. You may get some flack about only having 3 announcements, but most of the time they are already in the bulletin and people already know them. Put your announcements on PowerPoint slides as people are coming into worship. Use creativity. Remember the rule: 3 in 3.

- **80% rule**: If the announcement doesn't apply to 80% of the people in worship, don't waste everybody's time. Enough said.

Pay Attention to Flow and Transitions

Flow and transitions are things that worship planners need to pay attention to if the worship service is going to feel right in today's world.

Flow has to do with how elements come together and lead one to the other. It has to do with things like not asking people to stand, then sit down, then stand again in quick sequence. Bad flow. It also has to do with the emotional feeling of the different elements. You don't want people to feel like emotional yo-yos.

Transition has to do with the logistics of moving from one element to another. When Miss Emma reads the Scripture and then sits down, and then Uncle John stands up and walks slowly from the back of the church to make an announcement—that's a bad transition. When people speak, their microphone must be on. When there are video clips, they ought to work and start on cue.

The rule of thumb is that if there are 10 seconds of silence in a transition, you have lost the attention of the people. The more contemporary and/or creative worship services are, the more important it is for planners to give careful attention to flow and transitions.

Connect by Preaching while Walking Around

One of the most significant steps a pastor can take toward more fully engaging the congregation in worship is the movement away from notes and especially the reading of the message/ sermon. Preaching while walking around produces a stronger connection with the congregation where there is a sense that you are talking from the heart and sharing directly with them.

I am not advocating a lack of preparation here. I suggest that the preacher still develop a full manuscript so that the message is well thought out. The next step is to practice the delivery of the message so that you can do it without your notes.

Commit to Excellence

In today's world, especially for the younger generations, people have an expectation of excellence that is just part of the culture we live in. If what you do isn't done with excellence, then acting like it's just the church family can become a self-fulfilling act.

Think about it this way: Is God glorified by mediocrity?

Suggested Additional Resources for Worship

- *The Big Idea: Aligning the Ministries of Your Church through Creative Collaboration,* Dave Ferguson, Zondervan, 2007.

- *Taking Flight with Creativity: Worship Design Teams That Work,* Len Wilson & Jason Moore, Abingdon Press, 2009.

- *Missional Worship: Increasing Attendance and Expanding the Boundaries of your Church,* Cathy Townley, Chalice Press, 2011.

- *Toward Vitality Research Project,* Kim Shockley, General Board of Discipleship, 2012.

- *Growing True Disciples: New Strategies for Producing Genuine Followers of Christ,* George Barna, WaterBrook Press, 2001.

- *4MAT,* Dr. Bernice McCarthy, www.aboutlearning.com.

- *Worship Ways: For the People Within Your Reach,* Thomas G. Bandy, Abingdon Press, Nashville, 2014.

- *Building Worship Bridges: Worship to Accelerate Neighborhood Connections,* Cathy Townley, Kay Kotan, Bishop Robert Farr, Market Square Publishing, 2017.

Shift 3

From Membership to Discipleship

I have been crucified with Christ and I no longer live,
but Christ lives in me.
—The Apostle Paul, Galatians 2:20

[S]o that we may no longer be children. . . .
Rather, speaking the truth in love, we are to grow up in every way
into him who is the head, into Christ.
—The Apostle Paul, Ephesians 4:14-15 (ESV)

"Come, follow me. . . ."
—Jesus, Matthew 4:19

"Therefore, go and make disciples . . . teaching them to
obey everything I have commanded you."
—Jesus, Matthew 28:19–20

Discipleship Survey

The survey for this chapter will help you and your congregation explore the quality of your discipleship training. Discipleship is perceived in a multitude of ways, but this survey helps congregational leadership understand more fully if they have a path to spiritual progress which is understood and accessible by all.

(1 = Poor . . . 4 = Amazing)

	Intentional Discipleship	1	2	3	4
1	This congregation has established clear expectations for maturity in discipleship.				
2.	I am an active participant in a small group that includes fellowship, growth, and mission experiences.				
3.	At least once a year, someone from the congregation has a conversation with me about my progress as a disciple.				
4.	Our congregation offers a variety of educational experiences based on the level of maturity as a disciple.				
5.	I have spiritual friends, a mentor, a coach, or a spiritual director who holds me accountable.				
6.	Lay persons are equipped to lead small groups and serve as mentors or coaches for discipleship.				
7.	Worship experiences consistently lead persons to the next step in their discipleship.				
8.	The most mature disciples are encouraged to provide discipling relationships with those new to the faith and leadership for the ministries of the congregation.				
9.	I am involved in serving in the local community, making a difference in people's lives.				
10.	I take responsibility for my own spiritual growth through the daily practices of spiritual disciplines.				

		1	2	3	4
11.	I have relationships beyond the local church through which I am intentionally sharing God's love.				
12.	I give 10% of my income to the ministry of the local church and seek to honor God with the rest.				
13.	I have one or more close friends participating in worship and ministry with me at this church.				
14.	The church has helped me in understanding the Bible and how its teaching applies to my life.				
15.	The leaders of this congregation have such a close walk with Jesus that I am inspired to follow them.				
16.	I really feel like I belong to this community of faith. I am valued, loved, and engaged.				
17.	I am growing in my relationship with Jesus through my connection to this community of faith.				
18.	I have clarity about how God has gifted and called me to serve (made possible through a guided exploration process).				
19.	I live within financial margins in order to bless other people more.				
20.	This congregation helps beginning disciples learn how to pray, read the Bible, and serve.				
21.	Leaders for this congregation are drawn from the most spiritually mature disciples.				
22.	There is training available for this congregation in the building of healthy relationships and sharing faith.				
23.	There is a clear vision of what this congregation hopes for with every disciple engaged in the community of faith.				
24.	While a wide variety of classes are offered, there is also a core curriculum leading people toward the vision for discipleship.				
25.	I am discovering more and more the depths of Jesus' love and longings for me as a disciple.				

A perfect score on this survey would be 100 points.

When using this with your leadership team or congregation, here is how you determine an average score:

Total the points for each individual survey. Add the points from all the individual surveys together. Divide that total number by the number of surveys that were completed. This gives you an average score (out of 100 possible points), providing you with a "grade" for your congregational health in this area. Using a standard academic scale:

$$90+ \quad = \quad A$$
$$80\text{-}89 \quad = \quad B$$
$$70\text{-}79 \quad = \quad C$$
$$60\text{-}69 \quad = \quad D$$

What grade does your congregational discipleship receive? What did the survey reveal? What is your strongest area? What do you hope for in creating an intentional discipleship process? Write your answers in the space below:

Consider the following hypothetical story:

Jim and Sally are looking for a way to get connected in their new community. On Sunday morning they decide to start checking out the local churches. They visit Grace Church and really like both the music and the pastor's message. At the end of the service an invitation is given. People are encouraged to make a commitment to Jesus, renew their commitment to Jesus or, if they are ready, come forward and join the church.

Jim and Sally look at each other and nod. Then they walk up the aisle and became members of the congregation, giving their names to the pastor and saying yes to the stated vows.

In a church culture where the number of people on the rolls is the most important thing, this scenario might make sense. However, it might also explain why, in a large percentage of our congregations, only 25–40% of the membership actually attends worship in a given month, why so few people say that the church is relevant in their lives, or why congregations become focused on taking care of "their own," rather than transforming their communities.

Of course, most of our congregations don't just extend an open invitation like the one described above (although I have seen it done). We expect people to attend a 'membership class' before they can join. Most commonly, this class runs between two and four hours and includes the following:

- An introduction to the pastor, staff, and key leaders
- An overview of the ministries of the church and explanation of how the church can serve those becoming members
- A brief history of the congregation/church
- An introduction to the history of the denomination with core beliefs
- And (of course) a pledge card for financial commitments.

Again, in a church culture where it is all about getting people involved in the church and keeping people happy in the church, this all makes sense. This is a scenario being lived out in congregations across the country. Our membership emphasis has become more about joining and feeling at home in our club, rather than expecting members to grow as disciples of Jesus and providing them with the tools to pursue this goal.

Although, the way I read our mission statement, none of this misidentification of priorities makes much sense. Consider the words of Jesus:

"Therefore go and make disciples of all nations, baptizing them in the name of the Father and of the Son and of the Holy Spirit, and teaching them to obey everything I have commanded you" (Matthew 28:19–20).

115

Or the mission statement of the United Methodist Church:

"To make disciples of Jesus Christ for the transformation of the world."[1]

The church exists to "make disciples," not just members. So, what's the difference? Consider the following table and the distinctions made:

Members	Mature Disciples
Goal:	Goal:
Get people to join the congregation.	Create disciples who are increasing in their love of God and neighbor.
Church Role:	Church Role:
Keep the members satisfied.	Provide opportunities and relationships to foster spiritual growth.
Leadership Role:	Leadership Role:
Encourage members to be involved in church activities.	Encourage disciples to grow in obedience to God and service to others.
Responsibility for Growth:	Responsibility for Growth:
Church assumes primary responsibility for motivating people in their spiritual journey.	Disciples assume primary responsibility for spiritual growth as the church provides opportunities and encouragement.

One of the significant lessons I learned about halfway through my work as a "real pastor" (serving in a local congregation) was that to live out our mission (to make disciples) requires a shift in focus from membership to discipleship. Membership says, "It's about me." Discipleship says, "It's about God and others."

The recommended starting point for making the shift from membership to discipleship is to help participants make a deeper connection than coming and enjoying worship. I suggest three points of connection (often described as an assimilation process) that need to be in place before people are ready for engaging a more intentional discipling process:

- **Worship Connection:** The primary entry point into most discipling processes is the worship experience. Worship, as discussed in the previous chapter, provides the opportunity to connect more deeply with other believers, experience the tangible presence of God, be encouraged to take next steps in the discipleship journey, and experience personal transformation. Regular participation in worship is a key indicator that a person is ready for a more intentional process.

- **Relational Connection:** Discipleship is a contact sport. It happens in relationship with other believers. Small groups are the most common expression of relational connections (even if they are not specifically focused on the discipleship journey).

  It is recommended that every new person connecting with the congregation have a sponsor. This is an important relational connection to help newcomers find their way in appropriate connections and service.

  Sponsors can serve many beneficial roles for those they support:
  - Get to know the individual/family information
  - Discover previous (if any) church experiences
  - Discern passions for service and connect with opportunities
  - Understand development placement in discipleship process
  - Provide connections with small groups

117

- ∘ Make introductions to key leaders and staff

- ∘ Engage family members in age-appropriate ministries/ programs

- ∘ Encourage participation in membership class.

- **Service Connection:** It is important that newcomers begin to gain a sense of ownership with the congregation (that this connection is bigger than their personal needs). Service is how this traditionally happens. It is recommended that the invitation to serve starts with serving inside the church. This is less intimidating and provides the opportunity to build significant relationships with others serving in the same area.

It is only when these three connection points are firmly in place that persons should be considered for membership. The next step in the discipleship journey in that local congregation might then be participation in a membership class. I want to emphasize here that the membership class should be a stepping stone into continuing development as a disciple.

Earlier, we described a typical membership class with its focus on the church, its ministries, its doctrines, its founders, its history (as a religious tradition as well as locally), and, of course, its financial pledge card.

I don't think these types of membership classes are very helpful unless what you are looking for is an institutional commitment. If your goal is to help people make the shift from membership to discipleship, the membership class could focus on some of these ideas instead:

- Teach basic theological concepts pertinent to your faith tradition.

- Teach introductory spiritual practices so that all your members know the basics of how to have a devotional time, how to pray, how to read their Bibles, how to share their faith, how to live in authentic relationships, how to use the resources God has provided, and how to serve others.

- Connect persons to small groups if they have not already done so through their sponsors, or create a new small group with the members in the class.

- Clearly identify expectations of membership with a focus on development as maturing disciples.

NOTE: Participation in a membership class as described above should not be optional. Even those transferring membership should be required to participate in this class. Churches are filled with people who don't know even the most basic theological concepts and spiritual practices. This is the gateway into a commitment to discipleship.

For those seeking to join the congregation, it is important that the church provide clarity about the role of the church and expectations of members. This may require something beyond the traditional membership vows. In my last appointment to a local congregation, our leadership team addressed this issue by the development of a Membership Covenant. It included the following commitments:

- I will participate in weekly worship at least three weekends each month.

- I will participate regularly in a small discipleship group or other accountable discipling relationship.

- I will serve in some way in the local community (beyond the walls of the church) each month.

- I will commit to proportional giving to the ministries of this congregation and to moving toward a tithe.

If I were helping develop this document today, I would include a commitment to bringing someone from outside the church to events (worship, small group, attractional ministries) three times a year, as well as a commitment to build a relationship with at least three people outside of the church each year in order for them to experience the love of Christ in their lives.

As you have probably already noticed, these commitments are very consistent with, for instance, traditional United Methodist membership vows:

Traditional Vows	Membership Covenant
Prayers	Participate regularly in a small discipleship group or other accountable discipling relationship.
Presence	Participate in weekly worship at least three times monthly unless prevented by illness or travel.
Gifts	Commit to proportional giving to the ministries of this congregation and to moving toward a tithe.
Service	Serve in some way in the local community (beyond the walls of the church) each month.
Witness	Invite someone to come with me to church/events at least three times per year and build at least three relationships outside the church to witness the love of Christ.

The covenant agreement added some "meat to the bones," clarifying how our expectations were related to the vows taken by members of that specific congregation.

You may be wondering if there was ever any pushback about this clear set of commitments. The answer is yes.

I had a couple of times when, in a new member class as this was being presented, someone would say, "What if we're not ready for that level of commitment?"

My response went something like this: "That's OK.

120

You've been attending here for three years now participating in worship. I visited you when you were in the hospital. I performed the baptism of your child. You join us regularly for fellowship dinners and special events. None of those things required you to be a member. In fact, I think you'll find no difference between the way you are loved and cared for and the way those who are members are loved and cared for. Membership is not about how we will serve you. Membership is about a commitment to living as a disciple. The role of the church is to help you do that. It's about becoming part of a team (we call it the body of Christ) that is seeking to make a difference in our world."

It's all about making disciples. After all, that is why the church exists. It is our purpose.

However, while there is some specific discussion about building an intentional discipling process, the scope of what is presented points to the reality that everything we do as church needs to support the overarching purpose of making disciples.

Since our discussion is framed in this way, it is only fair that we share some perspectives on what it means (from my point of view) to make mature disciples of Jesus Christ.

Discipleship Perspectives

Discipleship is about a lifestyle of worship. In a world where we are encouraged to meet our every need, desire, or hope—placing ourselves at the center of our world because "We're worth it," discipleship invites us to discover that truly abundant life is the product of a life lived for God and others. Maturing disciples move away from "It's about me" and toward a lifestyle focused on God and others.

Discipleship is about relationships. Christianity is a relational faith. Our model is the Trinity. The Father, Son, and Holy Spirit are One God, so intimately connected that they are each the full expression of the other. As Jesus put it in his prayer:

"I pray . . . that all of them may be one, Father, just as you are in me and I am in you" (John 17:20–21), and "When he, the Spirit of truth, comes . . . he will glorify me because it is from me that he will receive what he will make known to you. All that belongs to the Father is mine. That is why I said the Spirit will receive from me what he will make known to you" (John 16:13–15).

Like the fullness of the relationship modeled in the Trinity, disciples are called to be in relationship with God (Father, Son, and Holy Spirit), with each other, and with the world that God loves. It is this calling that is expressed so clearly in the traditional communion liturgy prayer: "Make us one with you, one with each other, and one in our ministry to all the world."

Not only is discipleship about relationships, it is formed in relationships. The Scriptures are replete with examples of this understanding about making disciples: Jesus and the original 12 disciples, Barnabas and Paul, Paul and Timothy, Elijah and Elisha, Moses and Joshua, and the list goes on. These relationships are characterized by commitment to one another, transparency, discovery, encouragement, challenge, accountability, and love. They are models worthy of our focus and attention today as well.

Discipleship is about a process, not a program. John Wesley, founder of the Methodist movement, asked the question that continues to be asked of every candidate for ordination, "Are you going on to perfection?" By perfection, he does not mean absolute perfection (that only works for Jesus) but a perfect love for God and others. I'm not sure why this question is asked only to those seeking ordination, since we are all ordained by our baptism, and we are all called to move toward maturity as disciples. This idea of movement is critical to the process of discipleship. Discipleship is not a state of being. It is a process of becoming.

For the past few decades the model used for making disciples has been predominantly programmatic. Drawing on the work of Greg Ogden in *Transforming Discipleship,* consider the following set of distinctions:

- As a process supported by relationships, discipleship is about investing in people so that the life of Jesus is integrated into their being. As a program, discipleship is safe, controllable, and less intrusive. It largely values information over investing in people.

- As a process, discipling relationships have a full, mutual responsibility. As a program, one or a few do on behalf of the many.

- As a process, discipling relationships are customized to the unique growth of the individual. As a program, discipleship emphasizes synchronization and regimentation.

- As a process, discipling relationships focus accountability on life change. In a program, accountability focuses on understanding or retention of content.[2]

Discipleship is about engaging our world. Rick Rusaw and Eric Swanson posed the questions, "If your church vanished, would your community weep? Would anyone notice? Would anyone care?" These direct challenges became catchphrases for congregations across the country. The message is clear: The church doesn't exist to serve us. It exists to serve the world, and to transform the world.[3]

To be a disciple and to equip people to be growing in maturity as disciples includes developing a heart and passion for serving others. This may take a variety of forms. It may be a personal ministry to a neighbor, friend, or co-worker. It may be through participation in teams providing community service. It may be accomplished through leadership in community organizations or support of recreational activities for children and youth in the community. It may be through regular participation in short-term mission experiences for disaster relief or the development of physical support to third-world nations. It may be through providing financial resources to meet the needs of those less fortunate or for those serving others.

The effective, vital congregation helps disciples discern their gifting, passions, and calling for making a difference.

Discipleship is about becoming like Jesus. This is different than learning about Jesus. It is about transformation, not education. Real discipleship is about behaviors. Let's consider some observations about discipleship based on current research and my own experience working with congregations in transformation:

- Recent research indicates that there is little to no difference in the behaviors of those who call themselves 'born again' Christians and those who are non-believers.

- Young adults, in particular, have a very negative perspective on the faithfulness of Christians in reflecting the life and worldview of Jesus.

- The driving factors in maturing discipleship are personal relationships and accountable discipleship.

- The longing for a strong spiritual connection is significant in the culture as a whole. This does not get translated into participation in a traditional community of faith.

- The educational model coming out of the modern era has proved ineffective in creating real disciples.

- There is no "one size fits all" approach to discipleship. People have differing needs for relationships and accountability at different points along the journey.

- Discipleship is a lifelong journey. No one retires from becoming a disciple.

When coaching the congregation in the area of discipleship, all of these observations come into play. The goal is to help the congregation consider how it might support the development of mature disciples who reflect the behaviors and worldview of Jesus.

Over the years, particularly coming out of the modern scientific era, discipleship ministries have been based on the core definition of a disciple as a 'learner.' This was easy and convenient. We could 'teach' about what it means to be a disciple. So, the Church developed a very academic approach to equipping disciples. Yearlong treks through the Bible became the norm. For those who wanted to dig deeper, there were verse-by-verse studies of recommended books. Then we added themed studies around topics that could help people understand how to live as better disciples.

So, here we are in the post-Christian era, and detailed research has been done to see how all this focus on learning and teaching has worked (e.g., George Barna or The Fermi Project).[4]

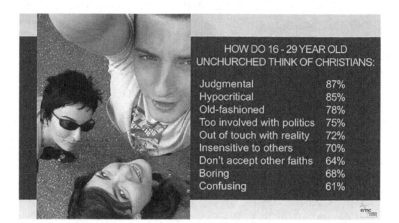

HOW DO 16 - 29 YEAR OLD
UNCHURCHED THINK OF CHRISTIANS:

Judgmental	87%
Hypocritical	85%
Old-fashioned	78%
Too involved with politics	75%
Out of touch with reality	72%
Insensitive to others	70%
Don't accept other faiths	64%
Boring	68%
Confusing	61%

The answer: It didn't!

We missed the part of the definition of disciples as learners that focused on actually becoming like Jesus, not just learning information about Jesus.

So, let's be clear:

- Discipleship is not just learning about Jesus. It means becoming like Jesus.
- Discipleship is not just about education. It is about transformation.
- Discipleship is not just about knowledge. It is about behaviors.

A Theology of Discipleship

Our mission is to make disciples of Jesus Christ for the transformation of the world. This clearly points us in a direction away from ourselves. That is very different from the idea of making members, where the focus is on what we get out of the deal: "What's in it for us?" and "How will you meet my needs?" The shift from membership to discipleship invites congregations to refocus our energies on our mission. The goal is the development of maturing disciples who are increasing in love of God and neighbor—growing in obedience to God and in service to others.

I suggest that discipleship be described as:

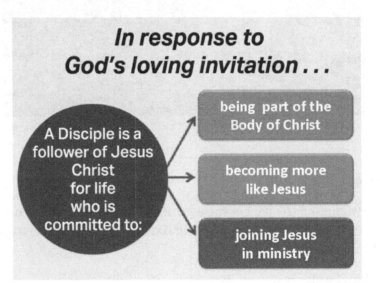

One way to look at this focus through the lens of Scripture is found in the familiar words of Jesus:

Follow me, (being part of the body of Christ)

and I will make you (becoming more like Jesus)

fishers of men (joining Jesus in ministry) (Matt. 4:19 KJV).

It is important to note that for none of these specified directives are restrictions identified as to how individuals will live them out. Discipleship is a very personal journey, and what works for one person will not necessarily work for another.

There is no "disciple-in-a-box"!

However, there are several dimensions of discipleship that relate to these three broad strokes identified in the definition.

The following graphic depiction shows another way to think about it:

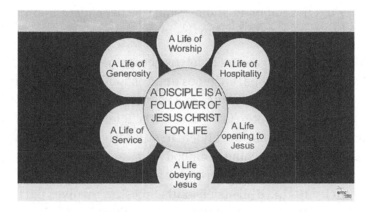

In **being part of the Body of Christ locally,** we live a life of worship and a life of hospitality.

A life of **worship** includes participation in corporate worship, as well as personal worship (e.g. devotional time) and even a lifestyle of worship where each action and circumstance becomes an opportunity to give glory to God.

A life of **hospitality** includes being part of the church community and welcoming new people to worship. It also includes our interpersonal relationships with and our acceptance of people who are outside the church and quite unlike us — even to the point of intentionally building relationships with persons beyond the church in order to embody Christ's love.

In **becoming more like Jesus,** we live a life opening to
Jesus and increasingly obeying what Jesus has taught
us. Together these reflect the concept of Intentional
Discipling.

A life of **opening to Jesus** includes not only hearing
sermons that teach the Scriptures, studying Scripture,
and reading Scripture devotionally, but also engaging in
those spiritual practices that develop our awareness of
the presence of God. As followers mature in this dimension, we take more and more responsibility for our own
spiritual development and become less dependent upon
the institution for our growth.

A life of **obeying Jesus** involves becoming more like
Jesus in our actions, attitudes and responses to others. It
begins with the acceptance of a relationship with Jesus
and a commitment to growth as a disciple. We not only
develop a Christian worldview in our daily living, but we
also increasingly come to embody the example and teach-
ings of Jesus. Jesus is Lord over all aspects of our life.
Maturity in this dimension of discipleship involves partnering with someone beginning the journey and helping
them develop as a disciple of Jesus.

In **joining Jesus in ministry,** we live a life of service and a life of
generosity.

A life of **service** includes supporting the ministry of the
local church with our time and energy and participating in
service projects sponsored by the church, but it also includes a
lifestyle of investing the best of who we are in service to others.

A life of **generosity** certainly includes presenting our tithes
and offerings as an act of worship, but it also includes creating
a lifestyle with margins that allow us to respond to the needs of
others God puts in our path on a daily basis.

As you probably recognize, these dimensions of discipleship

are directly related to the membership covenant discussed previously:

Traditional Vows	Dimensions of Discipleship	Membership Covenant
Prayers	Opening to Jesus/ Obeying Jesus	Participate regularly in a small discipleship group or other accountable discipling relationship.
Presence	A Life of Worship	Participate in weekly worship at least 3 weekends each month unless prevented by illness or travel.
Gifts	A Life of Generosity	Commit to proportional giving to the ministries of this congregation and to moving toward a tithe.
Service	A Life of Service	Serve in some way in the local community (beyond the walls of the church) each month.
Witness	A Life of Hospitality	Invite someone to come with me to church/events at least three times per year and build at least three relationships outside the church to witness the love of Christ.

Discipleship as a Journey

The Apostle Paul urges us to grow into maturity or completeness. John Wesley uses the language of "Christian Perfection."

Whichever way we look at it, from the very beginning, discipleship has been a journey toward the fullness of life that is offered to us in Jesus Christ. This journey happens in stages of development very similar to our life stages. In fact, this is the very language that Jim Putman uses in *Real Life Discipleship:*

- Pre-stage (not yet "born again")
- Infancy
- Childhood
- Adolescent/Young Adult
- Parenthood/Adult.[5]

It doesn't take a lot of imagination to see the connections to the journey in faith. In infancy, we are exploring everything.

The whole world is new, and we're amazed by what we're experiencing. Yet, we're not really engaged except to serve our role as cute and cuddly centers of attention.

In the childhood phase, we are totally into learning about our world. We don't know much, if anything, and someone has to guide us along, to teach us the language, keep us from doing things that will hurt us, and help us to develop in ways that will be the foundations for the rest of life.

The adolescent phase moves us into taking responsibility for our lives. We begin to establish some independence. We discover what works well for us. We make some of our own decisions about how to do life.

The parenthood/adult phase moves us squarely into the realm of focusing beyond ourselves. We realize that life done well is done so by helping others do life well. We continue to grow personally, but the focus becomes other-centered.

We use the language of Searching, Exploring, Beginning, Growing, and Maturing to describe these phases of development as a disciple:

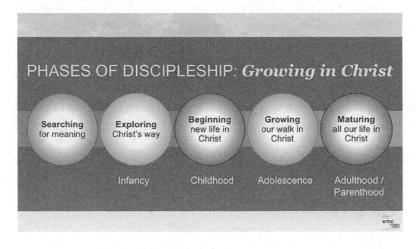

The phases might be described as:

Searching (pre-life in Christ): All persons seek to make sense of their life, asking questions like, "What gives my life purpose, joy, and fulfillment?" They may seek to fill this fundamental need in many different ways. (See Acts 17:22.)

Exploring (infancy): Although they may attend church and want to belong, but still they have not yet committed to following Jesus. They may wrestle intellectually with God's presence in their life, often with more caution than curiosity. The longer they attend without moving beyond this phase, however, the less likely they are to commit. (See John 1:45.)

Beginning (childhood): All are growing to understand and put their newfound faith into practice. Growth can be awkward. They are often vulnerable to insecurity and doubt. They are also the most excited about their faith. This is the largest and most active segment in church activities. (See Matthew 7:24.)

Growing (adolescent): Eager to be identified as Christians and going public with their faith, they are increasingly willing to take responsibility for their deepening relationship with Jesus. They seek to integrate their faith into life in a holistic way and look to Jesus to help them live their life. (See Ephesians 4:14.)

Maturing (parents): This group is moving toward complete surrender of their lives to Jesus. They exist to know, love, obey, serve, and be with Jesus. They also realize that the role of a disciple is to help make other disciples and live life with that focus. (See Galatians 2:20.)

It is important to note here that not only are there phases of development and that people in the congregation will find themselves in different phases, but also that the various dimensions of the life of a disciple will often reflect differing levels of maturity. For example, a person may have a great passion for serving others and a well-developed sense of calling (maturing phase for service) but may be in the beginning phase for opening to Jesus. They have made a commitment to be a disciple but have not moved into a growing relationship. Often the service dimension can serve as a catalyst for growth in other areas.

A friend of mine (we'll call him Jack) is an American contractor who lives in another country where he runs a construction business. Jack and I got connected through a seemingly obscure relational link through a mission organization (ReGenesis Ministries) for which I provide leadership. Jack is what one might describe as "a little rough around the edges" (maybe a lot!). He is a lapsed Catholic and former drug addict.

Yet, every time I take a mission team to that area, Jack takes the week off from his business and arranges supplies for the project, provides equipment for the team, and even trains the team for the needs of the project. During those team experiences, Jack also goes to church, attends daily devotional times, makes sure that we pray for every meal, and announces to everybody we meet, "This is my preacher friend from the States."

Jack is a perfect example of a person who is more developed in one area than in another. We suggest that you build on the strengths. With Jack it took several trips before he began to respond to anything 'spiritual' or 'religious.' Over the years he has come a long way. Now he even invites his friends to go to church with us!

Relational Support for the Discipleship Process

Discipleship happens in relationships! I'm not sure why, but we seem to have moved away from this understanding and substituted for it an educational model rather than focusing on the relational aspects of discipleship and supplementing them with solid Christian Education.

Jesus didn't say, "Take a class." He said, "Come, follow me." Discipleship is personal and relational.

The genius of John Wesley, founder of the Methodist movement, was that of building a process for discipleship based on different levels of relationship. The following diagram depicts that process:

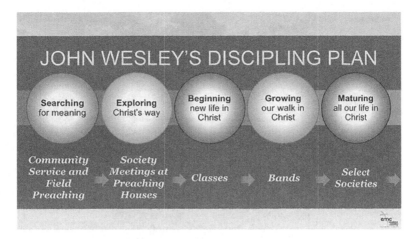

When people were exploring the faith, they were invited to a society meeting (basically a worship service) where they could come to an understanding of why it was important to be a disciple of Jesus.

As persons began their commitment as a disciple of Jesus, they were required to participate (if they wanted to be Methodists) in a Class Meeting. This was a larger group format led by a spiritual leader with weekly meetings designed to teach the basics of the faith and hold people accountable for their progress in living as disciples.

The most mature members of the Class Meeting group were invited to participate in Bands. These were much smaller groups (four or five people of the same gender) who engaged, under the leadership of a spiritual coach, in a much more intense focus on faith training and accountability.

The best of the Bands were selected for one-on-one training in faith development and leadership and were prepared to become leaders of Societies, Classes, and Bands.

The following paradigm provides a model for building the same kind of focus on relationships and accountability into our more contemporary setting:

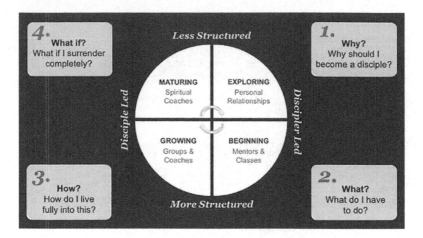

Let's consider this diagram section by section.

Note the two major axes. The vertical axis divides the image into right and left halves. On the right are found the two phases of development during which more support is needed. We call these "discipler led." This means, of course, that since people in these phases of development have not yet built a foundation, they will need someone to lead them—either through personal conversation or through a class.

On the left side of the image are the two phases of development that represent people who have built the foundations and are moving into an ever-maturing relationship with Jesus. We call this half "disciple led" because the support needed is determined by the disciple.

The horizontal axis divides the image into top and bottom halves. The upper portion is less structured, which means it is not based on formal classes or groups. The bottom half is more structured, which means that the disciples in this part of the journey are best served by a more structured environment such as classes and small groups or a formal mentoring or coaching relationship.

The image is divided into four quadrants, each representing a phase of development. Let's look at each quadrant individually.

The exploring quadrant represents people who are checking out a faith relationship with Jesus (see the discipleship matrix). They are usually asking some form of the question "Why?" or "Why does this matter?" They do not have a commitment level for participation in a small group and may not find the answers they are looking for in that environment, anyway. They are best served in one-on-one relationships where someone from the church (sponsor, coach, etc.) partners with them to help explore what a discipling relationship looks like and whether it is right for them.

Since those who are exploring the Christian life usually come to that point through relationships with those who are already believers (e.g. the story of Nathanael and Philip from John's Gospel), they need to be received well. First, and most critical is that a relational connection by someone besides the preacher is made. People want to feel like they could belong, that they are accepted. When they show up at a worship service to check things out, being received well includes the excellence with which the service is conducted, the relevance of the message to their daily lives, the preparation of the facilities to receive guests, and the witness to a commitment of this congregation to engage the community and make a difference.

In helping people move toward a life committed to being a disciple of Jesus Christ, research has shown that there are several catalysts that are most influential:

Top 5 Things Those Exploring Want from the Church as Identified by Willow Creek:

* Help developing a personal relationship with Christ (68%)

* Compelling worship services (68%)

* A feeling of belonging (68%)

* Help understanding the Bible (67%)

* Church leaders who model spiritual growth (66%)[6]

Questions for Leaders and Coaches
Related to Exploring Christ's Way

- How are newcomers engaged by someone from the congregation?

- How are spiritual conversations encouraged for the development of understanding key Christian beliefs?

- What system is in place to help newcomers find a way to serve in a ministry?

- How are new believers introduced to the practice of reflecting on Scripture?

- What kinds of opportunities are provided for the building of relationships?

- On a scale of 1–10, how applicable is the worship message to daily life?

- How does this congregation witness to its engagement of the surrounding community?

- How are members of the congregation encouraged to be engaged with those beyond the walls of the church?

- What support is offered by the church for inviting peers, friends, family, and neighbors to worship?

- How is the worship experience designed to invite people to take a next step in their faith journey?

- What is the practice of this congregation in following up with newcomers?

- What is the trend in 'professions of faith' for this congregation?

The beginning quadrant represents people who have made a commitment to be a disciple of Jesus. The question they are asking is "What?" or "What's it all about?" They are usually seeking help building the foundations of that relationship. This group is best served by providing introductory classes in the faith (e.g. Alpha) and foundational classes in discipleship practices (e.g. Following Jesus, Foundations, A Disciple's Path). Larger groups work well since this is primarily educational in focus. For smaller churches, having mentors from the congregation willing to work one-on-one with beginners in the journey seems to work well.

The beginning phase of discipleship is often accompanied by a sense of excitement as believers begin a new journey in life. It is also a time when there is a great deal of uncertainty about how to live into this new calling. The church has an amazing opportunity to help provide a foundation for this new life in Christ.

To help those who have begun life as a disciple move toward a deeper relationship with Jesus and a greater sense of God's presence in daily life, research has shown the following catalysts to be most influential:

Top 5 Things Those Beginning Want from the Church as Identified by Willow Creek:

* Help developing a personal relationship with Christ (83%)
* Help in understanding the Bible in greater depth (82%)
* Church leaders who model spiritual growth (78%)
* Compelling worship experiences (75%)
* Challenge to grow and take next steps (74%)[7]

Questions for Leaders and Coaches
Related to Beginning a New Life in Christ

- How does this congregation celebrate with people who have made a decision to follow Jesus?

- What kinds of connections are provided to help people discover what this new life will look like for them?

- How does the worship service equip people with tools for strengthening personal worship?

- What kind of training is provided for building the foundations of spiritual practices?

- How are people invited to be in some form of discipling relationship beyond the worship experience?

- What types of "on-ramp" service/mission experiences are available to help people discover the joy of service?

- How does this congregation help people discover their gifts and passions for ministry?

--- **Growing** ---

The growing phase represents people who are moving into a more committed relationship with Jesus. They are asking the question "How?" or "How does it work?" We have moved into the "disciple led" portion of the journey where the equipping of disciples becomes much more personal and individualized. Not everybody has the same needs. Some will want to explore more advanced spiritual practices, and others will long for a deeper understanding of how God is calling them to be in service to the community. In this quadrant we move from a one-size-fits-all to a more coach-like approach. Small groups tend to be the cornerstone of this phase of development, giving the opportunity for deeper exploration. We have also found that discipleship coaching is a powerful tool in working with this group.

Those in the growing phase of discipleship have begun to realize that there is more to the journey than showing up for worship and having a daily devotional time. There is a longing for a deeper relationship with Jesus, a stronger sense of the presence of God in daily life, and a growing commitment to make a difference in the world.

Top 5 Things Those Growing Want from the Church as Identified by Willow Creek:

* Help in understanding the Bible in greater depth (90%)

* Help in developing a personal relationship with Christ (89%)

* Church leaders who model spiritual growth (87%)

* Challenge to grow and take next steps (84%)

* Encouragement to take personal responsibility for spiritual growth (84%)[8]

Questions for Leaders and Coaches
Related to Growing Our Walk in Christ

- How is the congregation introduced to spiritual practices through the worship experiences?

- What types of relationships are available to support people in their growth toward maturity?

- What classes are offered that invite participants to explore the spiritual disciplines?

- How does this congregation connect people with a variety of service/mission opportunities?

- How are people equipped to use their financial resources in ways that honor God?

- In what ways does the congregation encourage cross-cultural and cross-ethnic understanding and relationships?

- What opportunities are offered to the congregation to develop missional connections within other cultures?

- Is there a clear picture of what maturity as a disciple looks like for this congregation?

Get People in the Word

As you may have noted, in all of the "top five" factors identified by Willow Creek, the focus on Scripture reflection was a significant component.

Regular biblical reflection is the vanilla ice cream of spiritual growth. You can put all kinds of things on top of the vanilla ice cream, but the ice cream is what builds the foundation. Notice that this is biblical reflection, not just reading the Scriptures.

There are lots of ways to encourage the reading of Scripture. Provide a daily reading plan (perhaps related to sermon/ message topics) for your congregation. Direct people to a reading plan through a link on your website. Provide copies of *The Upper Room* or another devotional for your congregation.[9]

Teach people how to have a daily devotional time that includes the reading and reflection on Scriptures. Basic tools like the Reflective Bible Study or Theological Bible Study methods are very helpful.

Start every meeting, group session, dinner, worship experience, or service experience with a devotional based on Scripture. Invite people to reflect on what God is saying through the Word about their lives, the life of the congregation, and their call to be the Church for the world.

Encourage people to bring their Bibles to church and to highlight, underline, circle, or make notes as God brings life to the printed Word.

Maturing

The maturing phase represents people who are moving toward being 'surrendered' to Jesus. They are longing to continue their growth, but also have a commitment to help others discover the blessings they are experiencing. They are asking the question "What If?" or "What if I became a fully devoted disciple?" They are seeking to go wherever God leads them. The strongest relational support for this group is the discipleship coach or a spiritual director as needed. This phase of growth requires much less relational structure.

In the maturing phase of development as a disciple, the focus turns toward equipping people to be disciplers of others. It is a movement toward understanding that it is not about me or my development but about how God can use the maturity in my faith journey to encourage and support others as they grow toward maturity.

This phase of discipleship begins the process of leadership

development. In Wesley's structural flow, this is where those who trained to be Class leaders, Mission leaders, Band leaders, and Society preachers came from. It is a solid model for the contemporary church as well.

Questions for Leaders and Coaches Related to Moving Toward Maturity

- What kinds of training programs are available to support mature disciples in mentoring, sponsoring, and/or coaching beginners in the discipleship journey?

- Who is available to support the continuing development of maturing disciples (e.g. discipleship coaches, spiritual directors)?

- What activities are supported by the congregation to support the development of maturing disciples?

- How are mature disciples identified and invited to serve in leadership roles within the congregation?

- What intentional training and equipping takes place to support the development of congregational leaders?

Developing a Core Curriculum

A friend recently admitted that if anyone in his church became a maturing disciple of Jesus, it was strictly by accident. I think this may be more of a reality in many of our churches than we would like to admit.

It is a fairly common scenario, when I consult with local congregations about discipleship, to be handed a flyer or brochure listing all the opportunities for people to participate in a class during the next 'semester.' The classes include a wide variety of topics. Many are offered because someone suggested a great new book, or one of the contemporary well-known pastors/ authors just released a new talking head series.

Little thought is given to "keeping the end in mind" (to use a well-worn Stephen Covey phrase). Yet, this is exactly where we need to start. What does a maturing disciple of Jesus do? How does the church help equip disciples to live in this manner? For example, if maturity as we describe it for a life of generosity means that we live on less than God provides (creating financial margins) so that we can bless others more, we will probably need to move beyond just telling people that this is what we hope for them. In a culture with rampant consumerism and materialism, the church needs to help people discover a countercultural mindset where they find their worth in God and not stuff. In a culture where people live paycheck to paycheck, regularly extending themselves beyond their means, the church has an opportunity to help people learn how to handle their finances in a biblical manner. Only then can disciples begin to live into maturity in a life of generosity.

We need to start with a vision for maturing discipleship and then provide the training to help people live into the vision. I suggest this happens when we intentionally design a core curriculum and set the expectation that all participants in the church will engage in this process. That core curriculum might look something like this:

Beginning Phase: A foundational course (could be the membership class) where all participants are introduced to basic theological concepts and foundational spiritual practices.

Growing Phase: Classes specific to each of the dimensions of discipleship in which you are encouraging maturity.

- A Life of Worship
- A Life of Hospitality
- A Life Opening to Jesus
- A Life Obeying Jesus
- A Life of Service
- A Life of Generosity.

The following are some possible resources that you might find helpful:

CORE CURRICULUM

BEGINNING PHASE

Suggested Training	Similar Kinds of Training Your Church Offers
A Disciple's Path by Jim Harnish	
Foundations: An Introduction to Spiritual Practices by Phil Maynard	
Beginnings by Andy Langford and Mark Ralls	
Alpha Class by Nicky Gumble	
Following Jesus by Carolyn Slaughter	

GROWING PHASE

A Life of Worship...

Suggested Training	Similar Kinds of Training Your Church Offers
An Altar in the World by Barbara Brown Taylor	
The Unquenchable Worshiper by Matt Redman	
Worship His Majesty by Jack Hayford	

A Life of Hospitality...

Suggested Training	Similar Kinds of Training Your Church Offers
Making Room by Christine Pohl	
Peace Makers Conflict Study	
Authentic Community by Jim van Ypren	
Connect! by Phil Maynard	

Maturing Phase: The training for this phase of development would be focused around leadership development and might include courses in discipleship coaching, mentoring, leading teams, administrative teams, etc.

A Life Opening to Jesus...

Suggested Training	Similar Kinds of Training Your Church Offers
Companions in Christ, available through Upper Room Ministries	
Celebration of Discipline by Richard Foster	
Devotional Life in the Wesleyan Tradition by Steve Harper	
Three Simple Rules: A Wesleyan Way of Living by Reuben P. Job	

A Life Obeying Jesus...

Suggested Training	Similar Kinds of Training Your Church Offers
Eat This Book by Eugene Peterson	
A Reflective Life by Ken Gire	
Disciple Bible Study, available through Cokesbury Bookstore	
Discipleship Coaching Training, available through EMC3Coaching.com	

A Life of Service...

Suggested Training	Similar Kinds of Training Your Church Offers
SHAPE by Eric Reese	
PLACE by JayMcSwain at placeministries.com	
What Every Church Member Should Know About Poverty by Bill Ehlig and Ruby Payne	
FIT available through EMC3 Coaching	

A Life of Generosity...

Suggested Training	Similar Kinds of Training Your Church Offers
Financial Peace University by Dave Ramsey	
Enough by Adam Hamilton	
Earn, Save, Give: Wesley's Simple Rules for Money by Jim Harnish	

Diagnosing the Level of Discipleship

In addition to the questions for leaders and their teams that we have already included, there are a variety of tools available to assist leaders in determining the level of discipleship offered within their congregation:

- *Discipleship Groups/Accountable Discipling Relationships Data:* The percentage of the congregation involved in discipleship groups is reported by congregations in terms of the numbers of people actively engaged in small groups. This data is often readily available, but a more accurate picture would also include those in accountable discipling relationships (mentoring, coaching, spiritual direction). While this is certainly not the only indicator of discipleship, this data does point leaders toward the health expressed in the most common form of discipleship.

- *Real Discipleship Survey:* This survey instrument is used as both a personal growth instrument and as a tool to survey the maturity levels of the congregation in six dimensions of the discipleship journey. The latter is helpful in assisting congregations to see areas of need that might be supported by the congregation.[10]

- *Congregational Survey:* The measurement of hospitality practices as perceived by the congregation is part of a more comprehensive survey of congregational health. This is included in the *Tips, Tools, and Activities for Coaching Church Leaders resource.*[11]

- *Leadership Team Assessment:* This tool is also found in the *Tips, Tools, and Activities for Coaching Church Leaders* resource. It is a set of questions for local church leadership teams to consider. The practices of hospitality, worship, discipleship, service, and generosity are all included.[12]

- *Membership to Discipleship: Growing Maturing Disciples Who Make Disciples:* I wrote this book to take a much more comprehensive look at the materials in this chapter.[13]

- *Creating a Discipleship Pathway:* This guide, designed for discipleship teams, takes a step-by-step approach to building an intentional process for discipleship.[14]

Most of these and other tools are available in our companion resource for *Shift* and *Shift 2,* called *Tips, Tools, and Activities for Coaching Church Leaders.* (See www.emc3coaching.com.)

Steps for Getting Started

In my work with congregations across the country, I have found several practices that are essential to the development of a culture of congregational discipleship. These do not represent the end-goal of discipleship. Instead, I have found that these are the foundations upon which a culture of discipleship is built.

Clarify Your Discipling Process

Creating an intentional process for growing disciples requires being clear about what a disciple is and does—and then designing environments in which people, with the help of the Holy Spirit, are most likely to move in that direction. Unless your church leaders know the goal and the route your congregation is taking to get there, the likelihood of people becoming mature apprentices of Jesus is slim.

To fulfill the mission of Christ, it is critical for congregational leaders to clearly and regularly communicate what they hope for each person spiritually. A pathway outlining how the congregation is prepared to support people in their spiritual journey is also important.

Suppose someone visiting your congregation asks you, "So what does it mean to be a disciple of Jesus Christ and how will this congregation help me do that?" What will you say?

Host a Congregational Information Meeting

It used to be that every church, especially in the same denominational brand, was about the same. Not so today— and that's good, because communities are so different. Many people have no idea what it means to be a Christian, much less a Wesleyan Christian. Many people have no more idea what happens in a church than most of us raised in the Christian church know what happens in a Buddhist temple. Guests need to get a sense of what your congregation stands for, where it is headed, and whether they personally will be welcomed. What does your congregation hope for them spiritually and how are you going to assist them to realize these hopes?

How do your leaders communicate the answers to these questions to people who are considering being part of your congregation?

Offer Foundations / Membership Classes

It used to be that you could assume most people understood the basics of the Christian faith. Maybe this was always an inaccurate assumption to make, but these days its inaccuracy is a documented reality. For example, the reason that many people don't join in the Lord's Prayer during weddings is . . . they don't know it! It is recommended that the Foundations Class be done in place of the traditional membership class. It is a starting point for those beginning the discipleship journey and much more relevant than the typical "get to know the church and denomination" class.

People don't need to be seminary-trained to be disciples, but there are some basic things they need to know and understand:

- What do Christians believe?
- How do I read Scripture?
- How do I pray?
- How do I cultivate a life of devotion?
- How do I relate to others in Christ?

- How do I manage my finances biblically?

- How has God wired me to serve?

- What opportunities are there for me to serve others using my gifts?

What does your congregation do to help new members learn these basics?

Everyone in a Discipling Relationship

While Jesus preached, taught, and healed among the masses, he poured most of his time into a small group of followers. The truth is that a small group of less than a dozen people who together are seeking to be Jesus' apprentices is the foundational relationship for nurturing spiritual growth in most churches.

Each group should share these priorities:

1. Developing caring relationships

2. Developing a closer walk with Christ through study, prayer, and teaching

3. Being involved regularly as a group serving beyond themselves.

Each small discipling group needs to have a spiritually mature and trained leader and to be using curriculum selected to advance persons in their spiritual journey. To support this process, if there are not sufficient mature and trained leaders, it is essential that leaders be in a relationship for development and training. This may be done by the pastor or by a couple of mature disciples.

Of course, small groups are not the only alternative for providing discipling relationships. Your congregation might consider one-on-one or triad discipling relationships, mentoring relationships, discipleship coaching relationships, spiritual direction relationships, or some combination of the above.

What percentage of your average worshipers is involved in discipling relationships? How do you go about selecting and training leaders? Would people say that being part of a discipling relationship is a basic expectation for all members?

Every Six Months, Help Disciples Review Their Spiritual Growth and Plan Next Steps

This may come as a surprise to many people, especially those who grew up in a church where attending several times a month, making a financial pledge, and being a decent person were about all that was expected (or hoped for). Our recommendation is that congregations organize so that every disciple who wishes has the opportunity to sit down with a more mature disciple twice a year for a conversation focused on their spiritual journey. "How is it going with you spiritually?" "How can we better support you as you grow to become a fully devoted follower of Jesus Christ?" "What are your next steps at this point in your journey?"

What do you think the effect of doing this for people in your congregation would be?

Close the Back Door

Some congregations are great at welcoming people initially, but very soon it seems these same people attend less and less, and then only at Christmas Eve and Easter. They have slipped out the back door—often because they didn't feel connected or engaged in the congregation.

Closing the back door may involve different things in different congregations. At the very least, it involves caring enough about people that you track their attendance and participation. If someone begins to miss worship, you can then contact him or her, let them know you have missed them and ask if everything is all right.

As you connect with people, listen for patterns that may suggest a problem in your discipling process. For example, one congregation began to recognize that new people weren't getting involved in small discipling groups where they could make new friends. Consequently, these people felt like they never belonged. The congregation implemented several strategies for helping people make the transition from worship to small groups. Another congregation discovered that newcomers liked the pastor but found that longtime members, although nice enough, didn't really make people feel welcomed.

Are your leaders tracking people's participation so that you can recognize if and when they are slipping out the back door? If you were to talk with those slipping out the back door, what might you discover is the reason for their disappointment and/or sense of disengagement?

Suggested Additional Resources on Discipleship

- *Simple Church: Returning to God's Process for Making Disciples,* Thom S. Rainer and Eric Geiger, B&H Books, 2011.

- *Foundations,* Phil Maynard, Excellence in Ministry Coaching 2014.

- *Deepening Your Effectiveness: Restructuring the Local Church for Life Transformation,* Dan Glover and Claudia Lavy, Discipleship Resources, 2006.

- *A Disciple's Path: Deepening Your Relationship with Christ and the Church,* James A. Harnish, Abingdon Press, 2012.

- *Disciple: Getting Your Identity from Jesus,* Bill Clem, Crossway, 2011.

- *The Disciple Making Church: From Dry Bones to Spiritual Vitality,* Gordon McDonald, FaithWalk Publishing, 2004.

- *Growing True Disciples: New Strategies for Producing Genuine Followers of Christ,* George Barna, WaterBrook Press, 2001.

- *Transforming Discipleship: Making Disciples a Few at a Time,* Greg Ogden, IVP Books, 2003.

- *Following Jesus: Steps to a Passionate Faith,* Carolyn Slaughter, Abingdon Press, 2008.

Shift 4

From "Serve Us" to Service

"Lord, when did we see you hungry or thirsty or a stranger
or needing clothes or sick or in prison, and did not help you?"
He will reply, "Truly I tell you, whatever you did not do for
one of the least of these, you did not do for me."

—Jesus, Matthew 25:44–45

The world hears the Gospel when it sees it, when its
witnesses are clearly committed to a more fully
human future, in this world and the next.

—Albert Outler, Methodist Theologian

If your congregation suddenly disappeared, would the
community mourn losing the blessings they provide?

—Rick Rusaw and Eric Swanson, *The Externally Focused Church*[1]

Service Survey

The survey for this chapter will help you and your congregation explore the quality of your service opportunities. Service in the name of Jesus can be a vague and hard to define concept. These questions make specific connections to biblical guidelines for serving others in love.

(1 = Poor . . . 4 = Amazing)

	Service	1	2	3	4
1.	I have participated in a discipleship process for discovering my gifts and passions for ministry.				
2.	Someone from the congregation has had a discussion with me about how I might use my unique gifts and passions in ministry.				
3.	I am engaged in a ministry beyond the local church which makes a difference in someone's life.				
4.	This congregation offers a variety of opportunities for me to be engaged in ministry.				
5.	This congregation offers a variety of opportunities for me to exercise my faith through ministries of social justice.				
6.	I have built relationships with those whom this congregation is serving in the community.				
7.	I have participated on a mission team for either a local project or a short-term mission trip this year.				
8.	During worship, this congregation regularly celebrates lives that have been changed and the needs that have been met.				
9.	I am encouraged to pray for the needs of the community around me and for the world.				
10.	This congregation partners with other churches and social service agencies to provide a variety of services to meet the needs of this community.				

		1	2	3	4
11.	My small group serves out in the community at least once a month.				
12.	There are regular testimonies during worship celebrating the difference this congregation is making in the community.				
13.	Our leadership team has done a demographic study to determine the needs of our local community.				
14.	Members of this congregation regularly interact with community leaders to determine how the church might best serve.				
15.	Our leaders model a life of service by personal engagement in ministries in the community.				
16.	This congregation receives offerings to support special needs in the community.				
17.	We track the service performed in the community to see if this congregation is growing in our 'heart' for others.				
18.	I serve in some way in the local community at least once a month.				
19.	This congregation has at least one ministry in the community that is a long-term relationship where the congregation is invited to engage and build relationships with those served.				
20.	Our leadership team has done in-depth analysis of community demographics to better understand the needs in the surrounding community.				
21.	Our church provides direct support for those in the community seeking meaningful employment.				
22.	Members of this congregation are encouraged to develop their personal ministries in response to identified community needs.				
23.	This congregation is known in the surrounding community for a ministry that is having significant impact.				
24.	I have participated in a short-term mission experience in another country or region of this country.				
25.	There are regular 'mission moments' in worship where the congregation learns about opportunities for service.				

A perfect score on this survey would be 100 points.

When using this with your leadership team or congregation, here is how you determine an average score:

Total the points for each individual survey. Add the points from all the individual surveys together. Divide that total number by the number of surveys that were completed. This gives you an average score (out of 100 possible points), providing you with a "grade" for your congregational health in this area. Using a standard academic scale:

90+	=	A
80-89	=	B
70-79	=	C
60-69	=	D

What grade does your service receive? What did the survey reveal? What is your strongest area? What do you want to hope for in service? Write your answers in the space below:

In 2004 I was living in Florida and serving a local church in the South Orlando area (near Disney World). After several years of little impact from hurricanes, it seemed our time was due. In the span of just a few weeks, the region was hit with three major storms back-to-back (Charley, Frances, and Jeanne), each of them crossing right through our community. Everywhere you looked following each storm, trees were down blocking roads and driveways, roofs had large sections of shingles blown off creating major leaks inside homes, and to top it off, thousands were without power.

In this relatively upscale community, people had often come to church with self-oriented questions: "What do you have for me? For my children? For my youth?" Much emphasis had been placed on excellence in everything that was done. After all, they deserved nothing but the best. (This was the Disney World area after all!)

The most amazing thing happened following the storms. With the power out in homes all around the community, a group from the church got together and fixed coffee and sandwiches to take around the neighborhoods. Teams got together and went from home to home to put blue tarps over the damaged roofs. Other teams got together and took their chainsaws and cut up the trees blocking roads and driveways.

It was a pivotal moment in the life of this congregation. It went from a perspective of "serve us" to service. That cathartic period jump-started a focus on ministry in the community serving those less fortunate, and it acted as a catalyst for the beginning of mission team support to other regions of the country, and eventually even to Honduras and Jamaica.

Service is about joining Jesus in ministry to the world, using our gifts and graces to engage others in ways that bring hope, healing, and wholeness to life. Let's consider some observations about service in local congregations based on current research and my own work with congregations in transformation:

- We live in a culture where, as Albert Outler puts it, "The world hears the Gospel when it sees it, when its witnesses are clearly committed to a more fully human future, in this world and the next" (as quoted by Lovett Weems).[2]

- Our mission is to make disciples of Jesus Christ for the transformation of the world.

- Engagement in the ministries of serving others is often the entry point for people (especially our young adults) into the life of a congregation.

- Many congregations—in my experience, a strong majority—engage in acts of generosity by providing resources to organizations while identifying them as service.

- Service is an integral part of our growth as disciples of Jesus Christ.

One of the realities of the *Toward Vitality* research done by several of the Methodist General Agencies is that most of the 158 congregations that were interviewed experienced significant positive change by shifting their focus from inward to outward. This changed the way the congregants related to their pastor (and staff), as they learned that the pastor is not there solely to serve them, but to equip them to be in mission and ministry. The shift in thinking also caused congregants to look at their community with a sense of God's purposes, identifying opportunities rather than difficulties.[3]

A Theology of Service

Rick Rusaw and Eric Swanson made the questions "If your church vanished, would your community weep? Would anyone notice? Would anyone care?" a catchphrase for congregations all across the country.[4] The message is clear: the church doesn't exist to serve us, it exists to serve the world—to transform the world. This shift from "serve us" to service invites the church to consider how this dimension of discipleship is supported by the congregation—from helping disciples explore giftedness and passions to providing opportunities for engaging in various levels of service.

For United Methodists this focus is built into the way we are to do life. In the Covenant Discipleship movement built on the Class Meeting covenant model of John Wesley, Methodists are accountable for "serving someone in need each week." In the description of the function of a local congregation found in the *United Methodist Book of Discipline* (Paragraph 202) we find the following:

> "Therefore, the local church is to minister to persons in the community where the church is located, to provide appropriate training and nurture to all, to cooperate in ministry with other local churches. . . ."

From the call of Abram to be a blessing to all peoples (Genesis 12) to the admonition of Jesus that when we clothe the naked, feed the hungry, and give drink to the thirsty, we also "do unto" him (Matthew 25), the people of God have been charged with serving those in need.

To be a disciple is to be a servant. To be the church is to serve. The church cannot be the church without being missional in nature.

Yet this service to the last and the least among us is greater than giving a handout. It is common to find congregations that provide resources to other organizations who serve those in need. We provide backpacks for children going to school, food for community food pantries, peanut butter sandwiches for children needing nourishment over the weekend when school is not in session, clean socks for the shelter serving the homeless, angel tree gifts for children at Christmas, and turkey dinners for those in need on Thanksgiving.

These are all worthy efforts, and we should support those serving the ones in need. Still, they are what I call **missional gestures**. They provide resources that are needed, but without our involvement in the lives of those in need—without "getting our hands dirty." I believe that every congregation should have a **ministry of engagement** where the congregation interacts directly with those receiving the services. We need to get to know people, understand their circumstances, be present to them, and be Christ in their midst.

I encourage all congregations to move beyond missional gestures (which do good and make us feel good) to finding at least one ministry of engagement. In a ministry of engagement, the congregation not only provides resources for those with specific needs, but also has direct contact with those being served. This approach fosters the building of relationships with people so that they may come to know the love of Christ. It engages our hands and feet rather than just our pocketbooks, and it helps us to grow in our understanding of the needs of those in our community so that we might address both mercy and justice issues. For example, a new church in Austin, Texas invites the women from a neighboring strip club to have dinner with them once a week. These women find a welcoming attitude, a good meal, and the opportunity to make new friends who know Jesus as a joy in their lives.

A ministry of engagement will change our lives as well as the lives of others.

Coaching the Congregation in Service to the World

When coaching the congregation in the area of service, all of these observations come into play. The goal is two-fold:

- To help the congregation consider how it might support the development of disciples who are engaged in service as a personal ministry, using their gifts and passions.
- To assist the congregation in identifying opportunities for transforming their community.

In Micah 6:8 we read these words:

Three things God requires of us: To act justly and to love mercy and to walk humbly with your God.

In this one short verse, the prophet suggests an outline for the work of the church. It also seems like a good framework to talk about the shift from "serve us" to service. Let's take the three dimensions Micah suggests and look at them in reverse order starting with "walk humbly with your God." I suggest this because this dimension of service forms the basis for success in each of the others.

Imagine a congregation where the disciples are walking humbly with their God. They are engaged in spiritual practices, living lives that bring honor and glory to God, building relationships with those outside of the church, using their God-given gifts and graces to serve others, and sharing generously the resources God has provided.

The disciples in this congregation know without a shadow of a doubt that they have received far more than they could ever give.

Their hearts break when God's heart breaks over the needs of God's people. They find joy in the very things that bring God joy.

They are walking humbly with their God.

This is the type of disciple that responds joyfully to a need that God puts in their path. They find purpose in joining God in ministry to a broken and hurting world. They are the first responders when the church takes on a big need in the community. This is the type of disciple that has a heart for those in need. They love mercy and do all they can to alleviate suffering. They are also the types of disciples that take a stand for those who cannot stand up for themselves. They seek justice.

So, we begin with *walk humbly with your God,* because without this kind of heart for the people God loves, one cannot really love mercy or seek justice. We might be coerced or shamed or bribed into dutiful service, but that is not the same thing as seeking justice and loving mercy.

The starting point for creating a culture where disciples love mercy and seek justice is growing maturing disciples of Jesus Christ. As was discussed in the "Membership to Discipleship" section of this book, as disciples grow in maturity, there is a natural movement from being focused on our own needs and desires and preferences to living life focused on the needs, desires and preferences of others. There is a shift from self to others. This is seen in all dimensions of discipleship. For example, in the "Life of Hospitality" dimension, the shift is from feeling welcomed and accepted to intentionally engaging those outside of the church in relationships where we are the presence of Christ in their lives.

This same type of shift occurs in the dimension of discipleship we term "A Life of Service." Maturity in this dimension is evidenced by joining Jesus in mission to others while using our God-given gifts, talents, and passions.

From a macro-level, the effectiveness of the discipling process in the dimension of service can be viewed through the perspective of the church as located along a continuum.

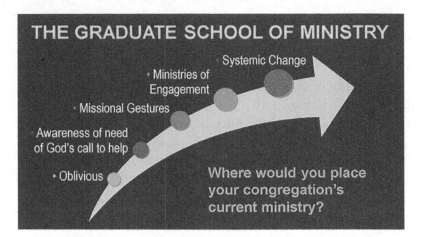

THE GRADUATE SCHOOL OF MINISTRY

Systemic Change

• Ministries of Engagement

• Missional Gestures

Awareness of need of God's call to help

• Oblivious

Where would you place your congregation's current ministry?

Hopefully, your congregation is not in the oblivious category, completely unaware or unconcerned about the needs of those beyond the church. More likely, you are in the category of the many congregations that have an awareness of the needs of the surrounding community—and even believe that they are called to make a difference—but are not sure how to do this.

A significant majority of congregations are engaged in what I have previously referenced as **missional gestures**. These are things that we do to help others, but without any relational connection to those we are helping. There is a long list of these kinds of efforts that I come across when working with local congregations:

- Food pantries
- 12 Step programs
- Meals on Wheels
- Operation Christmas Child
- Angel trees
- Clothes closets
- Backpacks for school children
- Peanut butter sandwich ministries
- Community Thanksgiving dinners
- School supplies.

The point of missional gestures is that they are good things to be involved in, and they make us feel like we are making a difference. However, they don't involve us in actual service. To serve means making the shift from ministry 'to' or 'for' to ministry 'with.' When we serve, we invest ourselves in direct involvement with people: we get to know them and become engaged in their lives. Much of what we customarily refer to as service is really generosity—we give generously to meet the needs of others.

This is a positive thing to do and much good is accomplished by it. Still, it is not the same thing as service. The congregation provides space, collects supplies, raises money, and serves meals. It doesn't get to know the people being served. Connections are not made to the love of Jesus that motivates the support provided. The congregation doesn't have any better understanding of the deeper issues surrounding the needs they are helping to temporarily meet.

As noted earlier, the next higher level of ministry is what I call ministries of **engagement**. These acts of service move us from passively contributing to the support of those doing hands-on ministry to being actively engaged in hands-on ministry ourselves. This is the level of ministry through which relationships are formed, needs are more deeply understood, and opportunities for transforming our communities are identified.

Examples of ministries of engagement include:

- Tutoring in the local elementary school
- Teaching an ESL (English as a Second Language) group
- Mentoring a middle/high school student
- Adopting a local school
- Hosting regular meals for the homeless and lonely in the community
- Hosting support groups for those in life crises
- Hosting an addiction support ministry (such as Celebrate Recovery)
- Ministry to fire victims.

The impact of ministries of engagement, in contrast to missional gestures, is dramatic. For example, at one church I served, we provided a weekly meal for the homeless and lonely. All of the food was donated by local businesses and prepared by our church members. There was no shortage of volunteers to cook and serve the meal. It started out as what I would call a missional gesture. We cooked and served. The homeless came and ate. There was little to no interaction.

We then made a commitment as leadership and staff that we would participate in the weekly meal, but not as cooks or servers. Some of us would eat the meal provided and sit at the tables with the participants and begin to build relationships.

We met some of the most amazing people! Some of these people turned out to be highly educated, while others had dropped out of school and life. Some were in need because of catastrophes life had thrown at them, while others had simply chosen to opt out of a more traditional lifestyle.

As we shared week after week, relationships began to form. We would greet each other out on the streets. Some of the participants began to feel so welcome that they started coming to worship and other activities. Those relationships began to open other doors to serve this group. I became the ex-officio chaplain for the group and was called upon to help those who were in need of medical care, to provide for those who lost all their meager belongings, and to pray for them in times of difficulty. When I moved to my next appointment, the homeless group presented me with a brand-new white shirt as a thank you gift. It is a memory I still treasure.

A couple of months after I moved to my new appointment, which was about 150 miles away, Joyce (one of the homeless group) showed up in worship. As she came forward to receive communion, she took my hand and said, "I just wanted to see how they were treating our preacher." Following worship, I tried to catch her at the door to the sanctuary, but she was already on her bicycle riding away.

Never underestimate the impact you might have through

sharing your life in a serving ministry!

The final, highest level of engagement ministry is that of being involved in changing the **systems** that produce so many of the needs in our communities. As Joseph Daniels and Christie Latona write in *The Power of Real:*

> No matter what the issue (homelessness, drugs, crime, etc.) the transformation process is started as some entity in the public sector begins organizing people for change. And the best entity to do this is the one that has or should have divine vision—the church.[5]

Rick Rusaw and Eric Swanson define justice as addressing the causes that create the symptoms/needs identified in the community. They suggest the following examples:

- Discipleship
- Tutoring/mentoring
- Job training/creation
- Livable wages
- Home ownership
- Ordinances.[6]

Several years ago, I worked with a church in South Florida that discovered many residents in the community were receiving fines due to an ordinance that required lawns to be maintained to certain standards and repairs to be made (e.g. a broken porch railing) in a timely manner. From a property value perspective of community leadership, this made all kinds of sense, but for homeowners who were elderly or of limited economic means, this policy was a source of continual anxiety.

The first response of the church was to engage in acts of loving mercy by sending teams to repair houses and get lawns to meet the standards that had been set. This was necessary since many of the residents were elderly or working poor.

Then the congregations serving the community (there were

several) got together and went to City Council to address the justice issue. They were successful in getting the ordinance changed.

Micah calls us to seek justice.

So, how do we begin to help our congregations make the shift to seek justice, love mercy, and walk humbly with our God?

Walk Humbly with Your God

As a general pattern for helping people grow in maturity in service in the community, I recommend the following three levels:

- **Expose Level:** This is the entry level for engaging disciples in service to the community. It is usually a one-time event with no long-term commitment by the disciple. Activities in this level are designed specifically to give the disciple a taste of serving. For example, congregations all across the country are conducting occasional 'Service Sunday' experiences. In place of the traditional worship service, these congregations do service as worship. Usually the participants go out in teams and are provided with a variety of low-risk service activities. This is often followed by a celebration gathering where stories are shared.

- **Experience Level:** This level of commitment is still fairly low, but it includes a longer-term commitment, with the disciple being engaged multiple times in a ministry to the community. This level provides the opportunity for hearts to begin changing as people discover the blessing of serving others. For example, some congregations take on the building of a Habitat House. The congregation raises the funds to support the project, and then over the course of many months, teams from the church gather to do the actual construction.

- **Engage Level:** This is a high commitment type of service in the community. Disciples are serving regularly. They are making this service a high priority in their lives. They also begin to mobilize others to support the ministry. For example, congregations across the country are discovering the difference they can make through an "adopt a school" focus of engaging the community. Through these programs, members often commit to provide tutoring for students or to serve as mentors for students over the course of many months.

Let's consider the image of a funnel as a way to frame the discussion and further identify how the congregational leadership might structure a supportive process for developing service to the community.

Personal Discovery and Missional On-Ramps

Let's start at the top. The wide part of the funnel is the entry point into a life of service. The idea is not just to get people involved in doing some kind of service, but to have them engaged in the service for which God has 'wired' them and for which they have a passion.

As part of the discipleship process, most congregations find it helpful to have some form of discovery during which participants learn about their spiritual gifts, their passions, their talents or abilities, their personalities, and their life experiences, all of which contribute to understanding how God might employ them in meaningful service. The two most utilized discovery processes are *S.H.A.P.E.*, inspired by Rick Warren of Saddleback Church[7] and *Network* from Willow Creek.[8]

It takes more than just learning about how we are uniquely equipped for ministry. I encourage congregations to provide a variety of entry-level mission/service experiences that disciples can try on and see how they fit. We call these *missional entry-ramps*. There are a variety of ways these can be created. For example:

- Some congregations build a mission component into their small group structure. Each small group is encouraged to take on a monthly mission experience. These do not have to be risk-taking ministries at this point. One group in my last appointment served ice cream to families at Give Kids the World once a month (a ministry that helps make vacation dreams come true in Orlando for kids facing terminal illnesses). They had a great time, made a difference, and were introduced to the joy of serving others.

- Many congregations have ministry partnerships with community organizations. Members are encouraged to serve once a month in any of the ministries as a way of exploring how God might employ their gifts (for example, serving in a community food pantry or serving a meal to the homeless at a local shelter).

• A third practice, mentioned earlier and gaining significant popularity, is for the entire congregation to have a mission experience day in place of the traditional Sunday worship service. The congregation gathers and prays, then goes out to serve the community together, and finally comes back to celebrate how they saw God at work. It is a great community-building experience for both the congregation and the community being served. There have even been examples of entire districts scheduling a mission/service Sunday.

Questions for Leaders and Coaches

Related to Personal Discovery and Missional On-Ramps:

• How do you encourage the engagement of your congregation in acts of service and mission through your preaching and teaching?

• What training is in place to guide your disciples through a process of discernment in their 'wiring' for ministry?

• How do you introduce your congregation to the array of opportunities to be involved in service/mission?

• Describe your theological perspective on the relationship between service (good works) and piety (holy living).

• How have you structured 'on-ramp' opportunities for those exploring the types of service that might be the best fit?

• What partnerships have you established with other churches, social service organizations, and local missions?

• In what ways do you lift up and celebrate the engagement of your congregation in service during corporate worship?

As the funnel begins to narrow, we reach the next level of involvement. This involves more commitment on the part of the disciples:

- Some congregations have teams that are engaged in a variety of community projects. The church might support a Habitat for Humanity project, provide home repairs for the elderly, or have yard clean-up for single parents. As noted previously, one congregation I worked with helped those who had been cited for non-compliance with city ordinances.

- Congregational mission trips are included at this level of commitment. Most congregations offer some type of annual mission trip (sometimes several) through which disciples can be connected to a more intense mission experience. Some of these are stateside, and others are overseas in focus. While all of these experiences help people in practical ways, the ones who often gain the most from the experience are those who participate on the team. This is often the entry point to understanding the significant needs that surround us, to say nothing of the personal impact that mission trips have on our own spiritual journeys.

For several years, I led and supported short-term mission teams in the Caribbean (primarily Jamaica). One of the most common responses from participants on the mission teams is, "I know we helped people this week, but we got so much more out of this experience than they did!" There is nothing like some hands-on experience to help people see the impact of the gospel message through the lens of sweat equity.

Questions for Leaders and Coaches

Related to Community Service and Mission Opportunities:

- How do you identify the needs and opportunities for service in your local community?

- What types of community service and/or missions does your congregation support?

- Describe the community outreach activities of your congregation in both missional gestures and ministries of engagement.

- What opportunities do you provide for short-term mission experiences, stateside and/or overseas?

- What is your goal for involvement in short-term mission experiences?

- How do you process the experiences of those participating in community service and short-term missions?

——— Personal Missions ———

The third level (narrowing) of the funnel represents the discovery of a calling to a personal ministry. This is really the goal for maturity as a disciple of Jesus Christ.

To be perfectly frank, this is a difficult concept for the Church to grasp. We are inherently institutional in nature and the calling to a personal ministry is not an institutional measurement. One denominational entity I worked with began measuring the number of hours congregation members served independently from the local church activities as a way of determining the effectiveness of the discipling process in relation to the service dimension. This was a huge and seemingly positive

171

step. Initially, the recorded hours of service included whatever and wherever the individual disciples did to serve others each week. However, a couple of years into the process of measurement, the powers-that-be decided to measure only the service done through "officially sponsored" service or mission activities done through the church. This, of course, returned service to an institutional focus rather than a dimension of personal discipleship. Ultimately, service is about personal discipleship rather than institutional needs.

One of the challenges congregations face is helping people understand the scope of things that fall into the category of personal missions. For example, I think each of the following qualifies:

- Providing transportation for the elderly going to the doctor

- Serving in a local soup kitchen

- Taking care of an elderly neighbor's lawn

- Preparing a meal for the family of a neighbor experiencing illness

- Volunteering at the local hospital

- Tutoring at a local school

- Providing childcare for a neighbor in the hospital

- Serving as a Stephen Minister to those in crisis in your community[9]

- Mentoring a group of middle-school boys or girls.

You get the picture! This is certainly not an exhaustive list.

One of the questions churches struggle with is how to measure the overall effectiveness of the process of personal engagement in ministry within a congregation. The reason this is important is that it helps congregations know if what they are doing is moving people toward maturity.

Some congregations use a service card that is placed in the offering plate during worship to track their progress. Others have members move a rock from one bowl to another if they have been engaged in at least one hour of service beyond the congregation. Again, we want to emphasize that the tracking is really for the church to determine the effectiveness of the process of discipleship.

This personal involvement level of commitment is also where the congregation is encouraged to become involved in justice ministries. Perhaps it is through community organizing to address a specific issue, partnering with organizations dealing with social issues, or creating ministries that address the causes of homelessness and hunger (jobs, interviews, housing, etc.).

Questions for Leaders and Coaches Related to Personal Missions

- How do you encourage the development of a personal mission/ministry for disciples in your congregation?

- How do you celebrate the involvement of people in living out their calling to serve?

- What tools do you use to measure the effectiveness of your system for developing a culture of service?

Love Mercy

Rick Rusaw and Eric Swanson describe *loving mercy* as addressing the symptoms/needs of those outside the church. They suggest the following examples:

- Providing shelter
- Feeding the hungry

- Clothing the poor
- Providing medical care for the sick.[10]

There are, of course, many other issues that come to mind when we start considering "loving mercy":

- Loneliness
- Aging
- Health issues
- Grief
- Addictions
- Divorce
- Stress.

What are other issues you could add to this list? Are there any that are unique to your community and context? With the abundance of needs surrounding any given congregation, the question becomes how do we encourage a heart for those in need and where do we start?

The following are some suggestions for connecting with the call to "love mercy."

To help develop an **awareness of the needs** in the community and God's call for your congregation to help, you can leverage existing interactions.

Preaching

A colleague, Jeff Stiggins, had just finished guest preaching for a local congregation on the theme of discipleship, which included the idea that serving others was part of our commitment as disciples. As he greeted people at the door following worship, one elderly gentleman shook his hand and said, "I just want to know when the rules changed. I've attended this church for 50 years and nobody has ever said anything about an expectation that we should be serving others."

I doubt that is entirely true, but apparently the theme of serving others has not been a major focus.

It should be.

Teaching

There are, of course, lots of great Bible study materials related to serving others. As part of the Christian Education support offered to the discipleship ministries of your congregation, it is recommended that courses in service be included. For example, there are some excellent books that could be studied, such as *Servolution* (a great resource to get people excited about serving), *Outflow* (five weeks of devotions and reflections on the topic of service, complete with a group study guide), *The Externally Focused Church* (a classic for anybody interested in this topic), *When Helping Hurts* (profound insights on understanding poverty), and *What Every Church Member Should Know About Poverty* (a must read for mission teams). Find details on these materials in the "Additional Resources" section at the end of this chapter.

Clarity about service as an element of discipleship

I recommended previously (in the "Membership to Discipleship" chapter) that a covenant be used for new members. This should include a commitment to service beyond the local church. I also think that it is important that a membership class include an introduction to serving others and identifying each person's gifts for ministry.

Community demographics

A demographic study is a great resource for helping leaders in your congregation become aware of the needs in the surrounding community. There are several companies that provide this service (MissionInsite, Percept). I use MissionInsite regularly. This tool provides, in addition to the general demographic information, the ability to do "opportunity scans" identifying people groups (Mosaic Groups), household types, and areas of poverty. The new Quad report, in addition to identifying religious trends in an identified area, includes identified needs for particular communities.

Community interviews

Demographic studies are very helpful, but nothing beats boots on the ground for getting to know the community. I recommend that the church conduct community interviews:

> Getting to know the community . . . personally! Interviews with community leaders are an excellent way to uncover where the congregation can build bridges into the community.

> Who might be helpful to interview? Think of persons who would be able to give you insights into community trends and needs. Think of all the local leaders who might give you valuable insights and provide valuable connections:

• Mayor	• School principals
• Council members	• Hospital administrators
• Police Chiefs	• Social Service agencies
• Fire Chiefs	• Pastors of other congregations
• Homeowners Associations	• Chamber of Commerce
• Realtors	members.

Praying for the community

Just do it! Encourage leaders and congregants to pray at every opportunity:

- Include community needs in corporate prayers during worship.

- Include community needs in the prayer requests printed in bulletins or church newsletters.

- Send email blasts for prayer when specific needs come up in the community.

- Encourage your congregation to include the needs of the community in their daily prayer time.

- Conduct prayer walks around the community and pray for people and needs identified.

- Canvass your neighborhoods and invite neighbors to share prayer requests.

Celebration of service opportunities during worship

It's a standard practice for congregations to celebrate the youth summer mission experience. For the churches I served, we would consecrate the team prior to the trip and allow time in worship for the youth to share about their experiences after their return.

I think the giving of ourselves in service is worthy of celebration when it's a major event or a team doing a local service project or even a family/individual that has made a difference in the community through serving others. These types of celebrations demonstrate that the congregation values service, and they witness to the variety of types of service people can do. It's a win-win.

A helpful exercise for assisting your congregation to consider the possibilities for engaging those in your community is to consider the human condition represented and current or potential responses:

	The Poor	Children	The Aged	Widows/ Single Parents	Orphans	Prisoners	The Sick/The Disabled	Aliens/ Immigrants
Physical	Medical Care	Flu shots, backpacks	Meal delivery	Lawns mowed, home repairs	School clothes	Birthday cards for children	Wheelchairs	Food, clothing, shelter
Spiritual	To feel welcome in church	Basic Spiritual Instruction	Church services in nursing homes	Small groups for single parents and widows	Ride to church or youth group	Hope, restoration, forgiveness	Prayer	Connection with believers
Social	Connected with others in the community	To be in safe, healthy environments	Companionship someone to listen	Companionship someone to listen	Big Brother, Big Sister	Visitation, watching out for prisoners, children	Care	Welcome into life of community
Emotional								
Educational								
Vocational								

adapted from the work of Dr. Raymond Bakke[11]

The chart is partially filled in as a sample. The same reflections could be done in the areas of social, emotional, educational, and vocational needs.

Seek Justice

To get a picture of the breadth of what might be considered seeking justice one needs only to turn to the social creed of any denomination. For example, the United Methodist Social Creed reads as follows:

> We believe in God, Creator of the world; and in Jesus Christ, the Redeemer of creation. We believe in the Holy Spirit, through whom we acknowledge God's gifts, and we repent of our sin in misusing these gifts to idolatrous ends.
>
> We affirm the natural world as God's handiwork and dedicate ourselves to its preservation, enhancement, and faithful use by humankind.
>
> We joyfully receive for ourselves and others the blessings of community, sexuality, marriage, and the family.
>
> We commit ourselves to the rights of men, women, children, youth, young adults, the aging, and people with disabilities; to improvement of the quality of life; and to the rights and dignity of all persons.
>
> We believe in the right and duty of persons to work for the glory of God and the good of themselves and others and in the protection of their welfare in so doing; in the rights to property as a trust from God, collective bargaining, and responsible consumption; and in the elimination of economic and social distress.
>
> We dedicate ourselves to peace throughout the world, to the rule of justice and law among nations, and to individual freedom for all people of the world.
>
> We believe in the present and final triumph of God's Word in human affairs and gladly accept our commission to manifest the life of the gospel in the world. Amen.[12]

Similarly, 35 denominations have affirmed the Social Creed of the National Council of Churches USA:

In faith, responding to our Creator, we celebrate the full humanity of each woman, man, and child, all created in the divine image as individuals of infinite worth, by working for:

1. Full civil, political and economic rights for women and men of all races.

2. Abolition of forced labor, human trafficking, and the exploitation of children.

3. Employment for all, at a family-sustaining living wage, with equal pay for comparable work.

4. The rights of workers to organize, and to share in workplace decisions and productivity growth.

5. Protection from dangerous working conditions, with time and benefits to enable full family life.

6. A system of criminal rehabilitation, based on restorative justice and an end to the death penalty.

In the love incarnate in Jesus, despite the world's sufferings and evils, we honor the deep connections within our human family and seek to awaken a new spirit of community, by working for:

- Abatement of hunger and poverty, and enactment of policies benefiting the most vulnerable.

- High quality public education for all and universal, affordable and accessible healthcare.

- An effective program of social security during sickness, disability and old age.

- Tax and budget policies that reduce disparities between rich and poor, strengthen democracy, and provide greater opportunity for everyone within the common good.

- Just immigration policies that protect family unity, safeguard workers' rights, require employer accountability, and foster international cooperation.

- Sustainable communities marked by affordable housing, access to good jobs, and public safety.

- Public service as a high vocation, with real limits on the power of private interests in politics.

In hope sustained by the Holy Spirit, we pledge to be peacemakers
in the world and stewards of God's good creation, by working for:

- Adoption of simpler lifestyles for those who have enough;
  grace over greed in economic life.

- Access for all to clean air and water and healthy food,
  through wise care of land and technology.

- Sustainable use of earth's resources, promoting alternative
  energy sources and public transportation with binding
  covenants to reduce global warming and protect populations
  most affected.

- Equitable global trade and aid that protects local economies,
  cultures and livelihoods.

- Peacemaking through multilateral diplomacy rather than
  unilateral force, the abolition of torture, and a strengthening of the United Nations and the rule of international law.

- Nuclear disarmament and redirection of military spending
  to more peaceful and productive uses.

- Cooperation and dialogue for peace and environmental
  justice among the world's religions.

We—individual Christians and churches—commit ourselves to a
culture of peace and freedom that embraces non-violence, nurtures
character, treasures the environment, and builds community,
rooted in a spirituality of inner growth with outward action. We
make this commitment together—as members of Christ's body, led
by the one Spirit—trusting in the God who makes all things new.

(used by permission, National Council of Churches USA)

It is a huge shift to move from "walk humbly with your God"
to "seek justice." The church is called to make a difference, to
engage the systems and practices that place people in need of
mercy ministries, and to engage people in ways that empower
them to live fuller, more productive lives.

As we noted previously, Rusaw and Swanson explain that
we are truly engaged in justice ministries when we are addressing the causes that create the symptoms. For example, a mercy
ministry would be to feed the hungry, while a justice ministry

might center around job training so that the person would not be dependent on a feeding program. A mercy ministry would be providing shelter for the homeless, while a justice ministry would be working toward home ownership.

There are an almost infinite number of ways that congregations could be involved in seeking justice:

- Many congregations have retired/active business leaders who would be amazing facilitators of training around developing resumes for those seeking employment.

- Skilled workers in a congregation could teach basic job skills.

- The computer literate could teach the novice basic computer skills that are often necessary to obtain employment.

- The church could serve as the physical address for those without the permanent address needed for employment.

- Transportation for job interviews could be provided.

- Addiction ministries could be provided.

The picture of the good we can do becomes more clearly focused. How could your church make a difference and seek justice?

Diagnosing the Level of Service

This service dimension of the life of a congregation is one of the most difficult in which to get any concrete data for analysis. Most congregations do not have any statistical measure related to service.

Some congregations (e.g., those in the Florida Conference of the UMC) measure weekly the number of people in the congregation who perform at least one hour of service beyond the church each week. A couple of examples of measurement tools were noted previously. The purpose is to measure the effectiveness of the system of service in encouraging participants to engage in personal ministry.

Communication Tools: A review of several months of congregational newsletters, worship bulletins, and the website gives a quick insight into the focus of the congregation on service and missions.

Interviews/Focus Groups: Discussions with individuals and/or focus groups will give great insight into the types of service/mission offered by the congregation and a deeper understanding about the level of engagement.

Real Discipleship Survey: This tool is designed for both individual use and as a congregational survey. It highlights the maturity level of individuals in several areas of the discipleship journey, including service. For congregational use, the survey is taken by a representative group and then averaged in each of the dimensions of discipleship as an indicator of the level of maturity for the congregation as a whole.[13]

Congregational Survey: The measurement of service practices as perceived by the congregation is part of a more comprehensive survey of congregational health. This is offered as a PDF download format which gives an analysis.[14]

Leadership Team Assessment: This document is a set of questions for local church leadership teams to consider. The practices of hospitality, worship, discipleship, service, and generosity are all included.[15]

Most of these and other tools are available in our companion resource for *Shift* and *Shift 2,* called *Tips, Tools, and Activities for Coaching Church Leaders.* (See www.emc3coaching.com.)

Steps for Getting Started

In my work with congregations I have found a variety of critical components that need to be in place to develop an effective culture of service. These do not comprise the service process, but they need to be in place in order for the process to be effective.

Identify Acts 1:8 Opportunities

A review of Jesus' words to the disciples in Acts 1:8 provides a paradigm for thinking about ministry to the world around us:

"But you will receive power when the Holy Spirit comes on you; and you will be my witnesses in Jerusalem, and in all Judea and Samaria, and to the ends of the earth."

In this approach, Jerusalem represents the people in the existing community of faith. What are the needs of that group? Judea represents the people most like the existing community of faith, but who are not being reached by the congregation with any significant success. What would it take to make a stronger connection? Samaria represents the people in the community who are very different from those represented in your congregation (language, culture, lifestyle, etc.). What would it take to build bridges with these groups?

Provide Missional On-Ramps

To reiterate a point made earlier, in order to help people discover the joy of being involved in service to others, it is helpful to provide what I call missional on-ramps. These are easy, low-commitment ways for members of the congregation to become involved. For example, small groups might be encouraged to participate together in a monthly mission project or service opportunity. The leadership of the congregation might arrange for a monthly community service project. These are also a great opportunity for building relationships with those in the community.

Encourage Vocational Exploration

One of the ways a congregation can help foster a culture of service is to help members discover how God has wired them for service. Having your congregation complete a S.H.A.P.E. workshop is one way to do this. Many congregations, of course, also offer spiritual gifts classes and inventories. Others make this a focus of their new member classes. Encourage the congregation to try out a variety of ways to serve based on what they have discovered about themselves. It is most helpful if there is some focused conversation about what people are learning about themselves and the community they are serving.

Cultivate Community Discovery

One of the greatest surprises for congregations and their leadership comes when they begin to discover who actually lives in the community around them. MissionInsite is a great resource for starting this process of discovery. In addition to providing general demographic information, MissionInsite helps you understand the characteristics of the people groups living in your community (Mosaic Groups), identify opportunities for ministry, and target specific age groups for ministry.[16]

It has also been found to be very helpful for congregations to interview community leaders (police chiefs, fire chiefs, school principals, mayors, chamber of commerce members, realtors, etc.). Asking about the needs of the community from the perspective of these people in the know puts a face on the demographic information. In addition, it creates a lot of good will with the community, but only if you do something with what you learn.[17]

Create a System for Helping People Discover and Make Their Kingdom Contribution

Many congregations are finding it helpful to build a system for helping members connect their individual gift mix to opportunities for ministry. Some have put together a listing of opportunities with a short description, level of commitment, and possible spiritual gifts that would be helpful. Others have provided this on their website. Some congregations have discipleship coaches who help members of the congregation explore options based on their gifting.

Celebrate Service

One of the most effective ways of encouraging a culture of service is to celebrate those who are doing it. Worship is a great place for this to happen. Having a service witness just prior to the offering is a way of acknowledging that our offering includes our time and talents as well as our financial resources. Invite people to share their story about making a difference through service. People connect to stories and may be inspired to see how they can make a difference as well.

Track Service

It is suggested that all congregations track the number of people engaged each week in at least an hour of service, which can be any way that people have met the needs of someone beyond the local church. This is a powerful tool to help the local church track its progress, to see if it is heading in the right direction. It has been said that we "tend to get what we measure." If the goal is to impact our communities, wouldn't it be helpful to know if we are making progress?

Suggested Additional Resources on Service

- *Servolution: Starting a Church Revolution through Serving,* Dino Rizzo, Zondervan, 2009.

- *Outflow: Outward-focused Living in a Self-focused World,* Steve Sjogren and Dave Ping, Group Publishing, 2007.

- *S.H.A.P.E.: Finding and Fulfilling Your Unique Purpose for Life,* Erik Rees, Zondervan, 2006.

- *The Externally Focused Church,* Rick Rusaw, Group Publishing, 2004.

- *MissionInsite* (demographic study), www.missioninsite.com.

- *When Helping Hurts: How to Alleviate Poverty Without Hurting the Poor...and Yourself,* Steve Corbett and Brian Fikkert, Moody Publishers, 2009.

- *What Every Church Member Should Know About Poverty,* Bill Ehlig and Ruby K. Payne, Ph.D., aha! Process, Inc., 1999.

Shift 5

From "Survival Mentality" to Generosity

The generous will themselves be blessed,
for they share their food with the poor.

—Proverbs 22:9

In everything I did, I showed you that by this kind of hard work
we must help the weak, remembering the words the Lord Jesus
himself said: "It is more blessed to give than to receive."

—Acts 20:35

"Earn all you can, save all you can, give all you can."

—John Wesley, founder of Methodism

Generosity Survey

The survey for this chapter will help you and your congregation explore the quality of your generosity. Just as we pointed out at the beginning of the first chapter that if you ask a congregation if they are a friendly and welcoming bunch, they will inevitably reply in the affirmative, likewise, ask a congregation if they are generous, and they will reply, "Indeed we are!" However, this area of discipleship reveals the greatest gulf between our personal concept of a generous lifestyle and a biblical understanding of generosity. This survey will help to clarify those perceptions.

(1 = Poor . . . 4 = Amazing)

	Extravagant Generosity	1	2	3	4
1.	Our congregation celebrates the generosity of members through regular testimonies.				
2.	I give at least a tithe (10%) of my income to support the ministries of this congregation.				
3.	This congregation provides opportunities to grow in the understanding and ability to be a good steward.				
4.	This congregation looks for opportunities to support those in need in the community.				
5.	Our tithes and offerings are received joyously as an act of worship.				
6.	Our pastor regularly preaches about financial stewardship as a spiritual discipline.				
7.	Our congregation conducts an annual stewardship emphasis that encourages members to take the next step in generosity.				
8.	Clear expectations have been communicated to members and participants about financial commitments to the ministries of the church.				
9.	The pastor is aware of the giving patterns for each family in the congregation.				

10.	As the offering is received, someone shares how the resources provided are making a difference.				
11.	A criterion for positions of leadership is that the person is tithing toward the ministries.				
12.	A biblical financial management course is offered as part of the discipleship core curriculum.				
13.	The congregation is encouraged to live within financial margins in order to respond to needs encountered as a life-style of generosity.				
14.	Persons are encouraged to eliminate credit card debt before becoming tithers.				
15.	A commitment of proportional giving and moving toward tithing is an expectation of membership.				
16.	Leaders in this congregation model a lifestyle of generosity through tithing and sacrificial giving.				
17.	This congregation provides a tithe or more in support of ministry beyond the walls of the church.				
18.	There is a sense of transparency about the way resources are utilized in ministry.				
19.	This church provides a budget that clearly articulates the support of ministries that align with the vision and mission of the congregation.				
20.	This congregation focuses on the needs of the community before the needs of its members.				
21.	The resources of ministries for this congregation are primarily (90%) funded through the contributions of members.				
22.	The financial support for ministries of this congregation is growing each year.				
23.	There is a clear sense of mission and vision which drives the financial decisions of this congregation.				
24.	The ministries of this congregation are led by members rather than staff, limiting the staff costs to around 35% of the budget.				
25.	A contingency fund of 5-6% of the annual budget is in place.				

A perfect score on this survey would be 100 points.

When using this with your leadership team or congregation, here is how you determine an average score:

Total the points for each individual survey. Add the points from all the individual surveys together. Divide that total number by the number of surveys that were completed. This gives you an average score (out of 100 possible points), providing you with a "grade" for your congregational health in this area. Using a standard academic scale:

$$90+ \quad = \quad A$$
$$80\text{-}89 \quad = \quad B$$
$$70\text{-}79 \quad = \quad C$$
$$60\text{-}69 \quad = \quad D$$

What grade does your generosity receive? What did the survey reveal? What is your strongest area? What do you want to hope for in financial generosity? Write your answers in the space below:

Consider the following: it is a real-life encounter with a medium-sized congregation. The names have been changed, of course, but if you have been involved with local churches for a while, it will probably seem instantly familiar to you.

Loveland UMC is a "county seat" congregation that has been in existence for nearly 100 years. For the past several years, the congregation has been in significant decline according to all the normal statistics (worship participation, professions of faith, participation in small discipleship groups, and giving). When the financial situation became the driving factor, the district supervisor suggested that the church engage in a consultation process to see what possibilities existed for moving into a more sustainable future.

While the consultation process covered the full spectrum of congregational life, in the area of financial support, the following factors came to light:

- The congregation had experienced a decline in giving of 50% over the past 10 years. There was a corresponding loss of worship participation during the same time frame, but slightly less dramatic.

- The average giving per worshiper had remained consistent, and in some years had shown a slight increase.

- The average giving per worshiper was at a level of approximately $1,250 per year.

- A significant percentage of the congregation indicated in a Discipleship Growth Survey that they were tithers, and many said that they gave beyond the tithe.

- The church has 'borrowed' from discretionary funds and an endowment to meet operating expenses for the past three years.

- The preschool run by the church operates at a loss, and the congregation makes up the difference. The church also provides facilities, utilities, and custodial staff to the preschool operation at no charge.

- Slightly over 20% of the revenues for this congregation come from 'rental income' committed by outside organizations which use the church facilities.

All or significant portions of this scenario are played out in congregations across the country, creating an unsustainable financial future for many mainline congregations. When this happens, there is a common response by congregations that is impacted little by location, brand, size, ethnic composition, or theological perspective.

It is called going into survival mode.

When we are threatened, as human beings and as churches, our survival instinct kicks in and we start putting up our defenses. We begin to circle the wagons, to use an early American metaphor.

When this happens, we start chopping at the budget. Usually the first thing to go is our mission support (both local and missional giving). Then we start to cut back on outreach activities (all the things that we do to engage the community). We start to focus on taking care of our members. We limit Vacation Bible School participation to the children from our church in order to reduce costs. We stop mailing newsletters to those who have missed church. We let the regular maintenance of our facilities and landscaping lapse. We cut the programming budgets for youth and children.

In short, we focus on staying afloat financially and taking care of our own. Of course, this begins a cycle of diminishing returns.

The process is complicated by what Lovett Weems calls the "Death Tsunami."[1] This phenomenon relates to the inevitable decline of the older generation that is currently the core of most local churches. The bottom line is that the strongest financial supporters in many congregations will no longer be with us in the next few years, and this will significantly impact the financial base for many congregations. Weems calls for a "financial reset" that must take place if congregations are to be sustainable in the future.

While congregations focus on survival techniques, rent their facilities to outside groups, take special offerings, hold rummage sales, cut staff and limit ministries to make up the financial shortfalls, the very thing the church is called to do—make disciples—goes by the wayside.

While Lovett Weems is right, and churches do need a financial reset, by this he means adjusting the financial baseline to a more realistic and sustainable level. I am not sure the answer is to circle the wagons, however. I think the answer is spiritual.

Extravagant generosity is about the spiritual discipline of

living a life with margins (i.e., living on less than one earns) in order to be a blessing to others. Maturity in the area of generosity is NOT the tithe, although for most people in our congregations, embracing the tithe would be a huge step. While the biblical standard for giving has been this benchmark 10% of our income (known as the tithe), maturity is about moving beyond this standard, living on less, and giving more to make a difference in our world.

Yet, one of my most significant discoveries in ministry was that the church cannot just state the biblical standard of a tithe and expect people to live into that level of generosity. They simply are not able.

Let's be really clear. Working with a congregation in the area of extravagant generosity can be very thorny. However, it is a critical area for the spiritual development of disciples and support of essential ministries. There are clearly areas where leaders can provide some clarity and a non-anxious presence. Asking the right questions can open the congregation to some significant insights.

A Theology of Generosity

We are called to be a generous people because our God is a generous God. Everything we have, everything we are, is a gift from God. It belongs to God and is entrusted to our use. Part of our responsibility is to use what God has provided, not just to meet our own needs, but also to meet the needs of those less fortunate.

This is true for us as individuals. It is also true for congregations.

We have been blessed to be a blessing.

The biblical standard for being a blessing is the tithe (10% as noted) of our resources. I believe that this is the minimum standard, even though this level of giving would be a stretch for most Christians. Generosity means that we will live on less than what God has provided for us, in order that we will be in a stronger

193

position to bless others through our generosity.

Practicing generosity as a lifestyle frees us from our dependence on finding our security in 'stuff' and from being enslaved by our creditors so that we can have 'more stuff.' The Bible is really clear that it is hard to experience the blessings of God when we're having trouble paying the bills for the things we can't afford.

Giving generously is not a way to get something in return, although I believe that God will generously provide for all our needs. The idea of giving in order to receive is not biblical. Generosity is motivated by God's grace, not the expectation of getting something in return.

—— Generosity as a Spiritual Discipline ——

Sometimes we seem to forget that our giving patterns are a spiritual issue. People spend where their hearts lead them. That may mean that the spending is all about them and takes the form of an affliction, identified by several authors as "Affluenza" (e.g., Adam Hamilton in *Enough*)[2] —it's produced by a common but unhealthy obsession with materialism and consumerism. On the other hand, our hearts may be led by the spiritual priority of generosity, resulting in our commitment to the biblical tithe (10% of our income) and even beyond, in order to be a blessing to others. It is all a matter of the heart.

We live in a culture infected with Affluenza and Credit-itis. Consider the following insights based on current research and my experience working with a wide variety of congregations:

- 82% of people in our American culture report feeling anxious about money.

- 65% of families live paycheck to paycheck.

- 32% of families can't cover a $5,000 emergency.

- 63% of families don't pay off credit cards monthly.

- 53% of families have less than $25,000 in retirement savings.

- The average mainline churchgoer gives 3% or less of their income to the church.

- Most churches designate less than 5% of their budget to serving the community or engaging in mission beyond the church.

- People spend 12–18% more when purchasing with credit cards than when using cash.

- The average family in American culture carries in excess of $15,000 in credit card debt, not including mortgage and car payments.

- The use of money is a difficult conversation for most congregations—people would rather talk about anything other than money.

- There is a prevailing idea that all churches do is talk about money, when in fact most pastors seem to avoid the topic whenever possible.

- A majority of churches do a minimal job of conducting a stewardship campaign. Only a relatively small percentage provide any discipleship training around the theme of biblical financial principles.[3]

Affluenza is a confluence of materialism and easy debt. Consider the following impacts of our relentless focus on materialism:

- We want more and more stuff because we find our value in the stuff we have.

- Our malls are the cathedrals of our culture, and advertisers are the priests.

- Our western rate of consumption is not sustainable. I recommend a great video, available on YouTube, called *The Story of Stuff: Consumerism, Capitalism, & Environment in America*.)

- "Whoever loves money never has money enough; whoever loves wealth is never satisfied with their income" (Ecclesiastes 5:10).

Consider the impact of easy debt:

- We buy more stuff we don't need with money we don't have.

- People spend 12-18% more when purchasing with credit cards rather than cash.

- Being in debt has become normal in our society, even in the church.

- Excess debt can literally reverse the Exodus and make people prisoners of living beyond their means.

- "The rich rule over the poor, and the borrower is slave to the lender" (Proverbs 22:7).

Some thoughts about what God wants for us instead of Affluenza:

- "Give us each day our daily bread" (Luke 11:3). Our material blessings are to be received trustingly and thankfully as gifts from God.

- According to Jesus, we need not worry about food, clothes, or shelter, but are invited instead to "seek first his kingdom and his righteousness and all these things will be given to you" since "your heavenly Father knows that you need them" (Matt. 6:25-34).

- Paul writes, "I know what it is to be in need, and I know what it is to have plenty. I have learned the secret of being content in any and every situation, whether well fed or hungry, whether living in plenty or in want. I can do all this through him who gives me strength" (Philippians 4:12-13).

- "Then the righteous will answer him, 'Lord, when did we see you hungry and feed you, or thirsty and give you something to drink? When did we see you a stranger and invite you in, or needing clothes and clothe you? When did we see you sick or in prison and go to visit you?' The King will reply, 'Truly I tell you, whatever you did for one of the least of these brothers and sisters of mine, you did for me'" (Matthew 25:37-40). God prospers us, not to raise our standard of living, but our standard of giving.

While the annual stewardship campaign with some mention of tithing seems to be the standard approach to "getting the heart right," the reality is this is not enough in our culture. The truth is that people don't know how to use their resources in God-honoring ways. It is not enough to tell them God's minimum standard is the tithe. We have to show them how to get there.

Perhaps even more important than showing people how to get to the financial stability of being able to tithe is helping them see the difference this sense of financial freedom will make in their daily lives.

In my last appointment in the local church, we realized that the standard preaching about the tithe wasn't sufficient. We decided to offer Dave Ramsey's Financial Peace University[4], starting with a group of about 10 people. Over the course of 12 weeks, these families (couples and singles) eliminated around $70,000 worth of debt. At the end of our first year of teaching people about the biblical principles of financial management, the giving level of the congregation increased about 15%. We credited much of that to helping people learn how to use money God's way.

Stewardship Should Be a Year-Round Part of the Life of the Local Church, not Just a Once-a-Year Focus

In all training venues we host—no matter the geographic location, no matter the size of the church or the age of the attendees—everybody always nods their head in vigorous agreement when this point is made. However, most churches still woefully struggle to have a meaningful year-round stewardship focus. Many churches continue to stick with the old-school model of publishing occasional financial updates and reminders in their newsletters, sharing an occasional finance update in worship or a word from the finance chair, then find themselves scrambling to come up with a fresh and motivational stewardship emphasis just in time to throw together a budget for the next calendar year.

Stewardship teaching done well is an integrated part of the life of the congregation and a regular inspirational reminder of the power of faithful people to do great work together when they use God's provided resources in sacrificial ways. The millennials are useful in helping us understand what this looks like from week to week. Since they are often cited as the biggest cynics when evaluating the workings of the traditional church (particularly regarding the intersection of the church and money), here's what they say they are looking for in weighing their investment in the work of a local congregation:

Transparency. All material related to church budgets and finances should be easily accessible. Every company that seeks investors out in the real world regularly communicates financial information to those investors (and potential investors). Financial updates should be a regular part of church life. Budgets should be published and available. Reports and budgets should be presented and written in such a way as to make their essential elements understandable to regular folks. Accounting geeks can tweak out on line-by-line printouts, but summaries should be accessible for the rest of us. This material should be clearly available online with a paper copy available for those who resist the web.

Immediacy. The church should regularly celebrate the impact of ministry and emphasize the symbiotic connection between ministry and regular giving. Rather than just announcing upcoming ministry events, we should recap them and share pictures and stories from them on ALL of our available media platforms. We should explain how these ministries change lives and communities. We should explicitly make the connection between generous giving (of time, talents, AND financial resources) to the success of those ministries.

Relatability. People like to hear about fellow disciples who struggle with the same challenges and perceived barriers to giving and yet find inspiring ways to live generous lives. We should hear first-hand accounts of people who choose to give, how they make the hard choices to prioritize the ministries they support, and how they grow because of those commitments. We should reinforce the scriptural message of the power of a generous lifestyle. (Consistently sharing these values requires discipline in planning by a team of people who care about this topic.)

Relevance. People feel useful when they are reminded how their sacrificial generosity makes the life of the church possible. Beyond special events and unique emphases, remind folks how their generosity supports the infrastructure of ministry. Not everybody understands the nuts and bolts of ministry and what it takes to make it happen, and a four-week campaign does not provide enough time to get into the details. By subtly working in such fine points throughout the year, people better understand the overall narrative of their power to make ministry possible.

Here are a couple of specific ideas that build on the above-stated concepts. First-hand accounts are powerful—the moments of sharing that many of us know as *witnesses* or *testimonies*. People are used to hearing clergy and ministry staff talk about giving and often assume that these ministry professionals are somehow in a special category regarding a generous lifestyle, but they listen attentively when folks just like them tell honest and inspiring stories. Most churches still have someone stand and deliver a live rendition of such stories, but we should be careful to set these speakers up for success:

- Give clear direction as to what you are looking for from a speaker. Don't just leave it open-ended. Share what you hope their story adds to the worship experience. Ask questions you'd like them to answer. Let them know about topics they should avoid.

- Have the speaker write down what they are going to say. This doesn't mean they have to read their story verbatim, but writing it down will help them organize their thoughts, stick to a time limit, and speak with confidence.

- Encourage them to practice. Either by speaking before a mirror, doing a run-through with friends or family, or doing a rehearsal with you or the worship team, they can benefit from the positives of giving their talk a test run.

- Supplement with pictures. If their story includes pictures they can share (and you have a way to share those pictures), they increase the emotional impact and relatability of the story.[5]

We often try to select people for these moments who have a good story AND a confident speaking style, but technology gives us more options to select people who are uncomfortable with public speaking. It's never been easier to do a video testimony or put a narrative video together, and these are demonstrably worth the effort. (Among other things, such videos can be re-purposed on multiple media platforms: they're not limited only to worship.) If you want to have a person live during worship, but want to have more control over the scenario, a great strategy is to do a guided interview.

There are also a variety of excellent resources to assist your congregation in becoming financially healthy.

Resources for Teaching

Here is a selection of the growing collection of excellent small group tools for teaching people how to become financially healthy, biblically speaking. After looking over most of these, it seems to me that the basic message is quite similar, but the style, tone and mode of presentation vary considerably. Leaders might want to explore several resources and decide which of them best fits their context and needs.

Financial Peace University: With wide appeal to both churched and unchurched persons struggling with out-of-balance finances, Financial Peace University is part of the array of resources offered by Dave Ramsey. In addition to radio, TV, and community event formats, there is a 13-week video series designed for small group use in congregations. Ramsey approaches financial peace from a biblical perspective. For information, go to http://www.daveramsey.com/fpu/home/.

Journey to True Financial Freedom Seminar: This is the most popular church seminar sponsored by Crown Financial Ministries. Crown continues to develop a variety of resources for different contexts and learning styles. For information go to http//www.crown.org.

Good Sense Budget Course: Willow Creek Church says that perhaps this six-hour course should have been named, "Principles and Practices for God-honoring Money Management." It teaches biblical principles of money management and basic tools for implementing them in daily life. For information go to http://www.goodsenseministry.com/.

Managing Our Finances God's Way: Part of Saddleback's Focus Series, developed in partnership with Crown Ministries, Purpose Driven Ministries and Pastor Rick Warren, this seven-week, video-based, small group study on biblical financial management can be used either individually or in a small group setting. For information go to https://store.pastors.com/collections/stewardship-resources.

Generous Giving: A privately funded ministry that seeks to encourage givers of all income levels to experience the joy of giving and to embrace a lifestyle of generosity. They offer a large array of online resources at: http://www.generousgiving.org/. Generous Giving has also sponsored national conventions on cultivating generous giving at which speakers from around the country address the topic. Many speeches are available on video and audio.

Questions for Leaders and Coaches

Related to Generosity as a Spiritual Discipline:

- How does your discipleship process encourage maturity in the area of extravagant generosity?

- What clear vision is presented to your congregation about what God wants for their lives financially?

- What support is provided to help disciples learn biblical principles of financial stewardship?

- What expectations are communicated to new members regarding their financial commitment to the church?

Preaching about Generosity

It is often referenced that Jesus talked more about money than any other topic, even love. If we are faithful to the Scriptures, we also help people understand the hold money can have on their lives and the freedom of living without the bondage of debt.

Certainly, I support the value of an annual stewardship emphasis. I also believe that preaching about the use of our financial resources should be fare that is more consistently featured on the preaching menu. This does not mean that we have to do a message on tithing every month! It does mean that the theme of financial stewardship can be woven as a subtext into a wide variety of message themes.

Perhaps more important than preaching about what God wants from us is preaching about what God wants for us (an often quoted insight from Andy Stanley). In a culture where people are valued for what they have, we have a message of being valued for who we are. In a culture where security is found in the stuff we have, we have a message of security found in our relationship with Jesus. In a culture where bondage to creditors is a way of life, we have a message of freedom from bondage.

Questions for Leaders and Coaches Related to Preaching about Generosity

- How is your congregation encouraged to be extravagantly generous in supporting ministry through a stewardship campaign?

- What is your congregation's attitude toward preaching about financial stewardship?

- How does your congregation address financial stewardship as a spiritual discipline?

——— Generosity as Pastoral Care ———

In my early ministry I bought into the idea that the pastor should not know how much people gave to the church. At the core of this premise was the possibility that by knowing the giving levels, the degree of pastoral care would be influenced. In other words, I would be more attentive to the needs of those who were the biggest givers.

I have made an about-face on this. I now believe that it is important for the pastor to know the giving levels of every family in the congregation. There are several reasons for this:

- Since the use of financial resources is a spiritual issue, the giving level is one indicator of progress toward maturity as a disciple of Jesus Christ.

- If there is a dramatic change in the giving levels of a family/ person, it may be an indicator that there is some pastoral care issue that needs attention.

- A dramatic change in the giving levels of a family/person may be the first indication of an issue between them and the church that needs to be addressed.

- The giving level of a family/person should be part of a semi-annual pastoral conversation about how the church might support their continuing spiritual development.

Questions for Leaders and Coaches Related to Extravagant Generosity and Pastoral Care

- How is giving tracked?
- At what point is the pastor alerted when there are dramatic changes in giving levels of a family or person?

—— Celebrating Extravagant Generosity ——

Congregations have a variety of ways in which they might celebrate the generosity of those supporting the ministries. The most common, of course, is the presentation of the offering as the Doxology is sung and then a prayer of blessing and thanksgiving is offered. Some congregations are more creative in the presentation, with clapping and singing and whooping and hollering in celebration of the faithfulness of God. Your congregation will need to find what works best in your context.

It is important to do more than just receive the offering, no matter what form that takes. For example, there is nothing more powerful than the testimony of a disciple who has discovered the blessing of tithing and the difference it is making in his or her life or a witness from a family that has overcome the bondage of debt and is experiencing the freedom to give and bless others.

The offering slot in the worship experience is a great time to recognize those who are giving not only their financial support, but also their time and talents to make a difference in the community.

Testimonies from those whose lives have been impacted by the ministries of the congregation are a great way to help people connect the dots between the gifts they offer and the lives that are changed because of their support.

Of course, celebrating extravagant generosity is not limited to acts of worship. A simple handwritten note thanking people for their faithfulness and generosity goes a long way. Taking extravagant givers to lunch to express appreciation is a wonderful gesture and strong motivator.

Questions for Leaders and Coaches

Related to Celebrating Extravagant Generosity:

- How is the celebration of extravagant generosity built into the structure of your worship experience?
- What personal touches are part of your celebration of extravagant generosity?

The Role of Leadership

I sat in a meeting with a group of leaders from a long-established downtown congregation. This team was seeking to move the congregation to the next level in worship participation and ministry. The theme for the evening was extravagant generosity. During a discussion about faithful discipleship in this area, the Council Chair made the following statement: "I don't think we should have to tithe anymore because we pay so much in taxes, and that is so the government can take care of people." After a moment of disbelief that someone had actually voiced such an immature thought, especially someone in a significant leadership role, I responded: "Well, Jim (not his actual name), let me just quote a Scripture for you—'Give back to Caesar what is Caesar's and to God what is God's'" (Mark 12:17).

At that moment, it became clear to me where many of the congregation's issues were coming from!

It is often said that "as the leaders go, so goes the congregation." I think this is particularly true in the spiritual discipline of extravagant generosity. Congregations are encouraged to make maturity in the discipline of extravagant generosity part of the leadership selection process. To be abundantly clear, it should go like this: To be an elected leader in a congregation, the person must be tithing or moving toward a tithe. The spiritual maturity of the congregation is driven by the spiritual maturity of the leadership, including on attitudes about generosity.

This expectation makes great sense when you consider the types of decisions that must be made by the leadership team. How will we best use the resources that God has provided to be about the Kingdom work? What kinds of ministries will accomplish God's purposes for this congregation? Do we invest in caring for ourselves and "our people," or do we invest in the community around us? What percentage of our resources will we spend on bricks and mortar and programming, and what will we spend in our mission to transform the world? How will our facilities be used to support the work God is doing in our community?

These types of questions drive the direction of congregational ministries and impact. Do we really want immature believers making these decisions?

It is also important for the congregation to trust leadership to be open and transparent about the way in which finances are handled. There are a variety of factors at play:

- Is there a budget built around the needs and vision of the congregation?

- Is the vision communicated clearly during a stewardship campaign, giving people the opportunity to support the vision?

- Are regular financial reports prepared and available to the congregation?

- Is the congregation made aware of financial challenges and what leadership is doing to meet them?

- Are there policies that leadership follows to avoid debt and to avoid spending all resources on themselves?

It is worth noting here that those congregations who have done the work of positive change that has resulted in a more outward-focused mission and ministry are also reaping the benefit of more meaningful support. Very few of the congregations interviewed for *Toward Vitality* (the previously cited United Methodist denominational study) reported financial difficulties.[6] These congregations were willing to give generously to a sense of vision and purpose that came from a sense of God's purpose for that congregation within its community.

Church Structures that Support Generosity

Keeping the Main Stream the Main Stream

Okay, just a little play on words that alludes to Stephen Covey's famous admonition to "keep the main thing the main thing," but it's an important one. I work with churches that build budgets around not only the expected level of giving by the congregation, but anticipated facility rental income, fund-raisers (bake sales, rummage sales etc.), and preschool income. Some are staying afloat based on the income from endowments.

In general, these supplemental income strategies are risky. In my consultation work with congregations, a projected revenue of 20% or more from any of these areas is a red flag. These revenue sources are too undependable. Additionally, they are not biblical in nature.

The church should focus on creating a strong sense of generosity rather than on ways to supplement giving to meet the needs of the congregation. Gary McIntosh and Charles Arn identify five motivations (or as they say, "pockets") for giving:

1. **The bill pocket:** giving to the general fund to help the church pay its bills.

2. **The missions pocket:** giving to support the work of missionaries, the mission work of the denomination, and local mission and outreach.

3. **The education pocket:** giving to support universities, colleges, and seminaries. This giving can also be called upon for educational support in the local church like scholarships, computers, and educational programming.

4. **The benevolence pocket:** giving to the poor and needy. These resources can often be counted on for local food banks, shelters, and medical clinics supported by the congregation.

5. **The building pocket:** giving for the brick and mortar facilities.[7]

If these are the five motivators for giving, the question for the local church becomes how the opportunities for giving might be framed to encourage generosity.

Discernment, not Preferences

As noted previously, people respond generously when there is a strong vision for the difference the giving can make in the community and world.

The vision must be focused on what God wants and not on what the people would like to have or do. It requires faith to

208

move forward, because it is bigger than what the congregation could do on its own. It creates extended community in relationship with each other and with God. In addition, it relies on the Holy Spirit for guidance.

Model Generosity

If a church really wants to get people excited about generosity, it must model generosity. The most successful congregations are those which literally give themselves away. The focus becomes "what difference can we make?" rather than "how can we support our programs?"

I believe that every church ought to be at least a tithing church. That means that 10% of the revenues are designated for making a difference in our community (and in this community tithe calculation, I am not including denominational obligations).

I was recently working with a congregation that has been slowly declining for about 20 years. It is disengaged from the community. There is no service done in and with the local community. Worship participants drive into the community and then leave with no continued connection. The budget reflects community support of 0.03%. Nearly 100% of giving is used to take care of their own.

Contrast this with a congregation that has grown from 50 to over 1,000 in weekly worship participation primarily due to giving itself away. People are drawn to ministries that demonstrate the love of Jesus through their generosity.

Budgets

I have worked with a surprising number of congregations (most smaller) that have no budget in place. They just try to make sure they don't spend more than they take in. While I applaud the stewardship focus of living within their means, I also believe that a budget would be helpful.

Why church budgets?

- Budgets show the allocation of resources.

- They are used to authorize action.

- Budgets provide boundaries and benchmarks.

- Budgets are tools that help financial leaders.

What budgets don't do:

- They don't motivate people to give.

- They don't communicate priorities and missional engagement.

- They don't connect viscerally with the reasons that people give.

People do not give to budgets. They give less from the head than from the heart. People give to other people, to needs, to causes—to things that make them feel good and happy.

So, what can you expect in terms of giving levels? As a general rule, you can expect about $20 per person in worship each week or $1,000 per person in worship each year. Of course, the better job the congregation does of casting a vision and inviting people to connect resources from each of their "pockets" to opportunities in the church, the stronger this giving level will be.

Some guidelines for budgets:

- A general guideline of 33/33/33 is suggested as a starting point for most budgets: 33% to staff, 33% to programs/worship, 33% for facilities/utilities/maintenance.

- Staff costs usually range from 35-50% in the local church budget (33% is recommended).

- Most churches maintain a contingency fund of 5-6%.

It is recommended that congregations make a shift from traditional to narrative budgets (traditional budgets featuring line items and interminable columns of figures). Narrative budgets, which tell the story of how financial resources will be used to support ministry, are far superior in helping people understand what happens to the money they give:

> The narrative budget is one way to give people—especially those in leadership positions—an opportunity to experience the mission and ministry that are achieved through the various line items. It focuses less on the financial numbers and more on what the income accomplishes. It is a one to two-page presentation that explains: (1) what the church hopes to accomplish and (2) why the funding is needed to reach and exceed its goals.[8]

While the narrative budget can be presented with just words (as in the examples you can find on the UM Discipleship Ministries website), it is even better to include pictures and graphics. Several nice examples can be found at Centerforfaithandgiving.org (enter "Narrative Budget" in the search box and then select "Narrative Budget Examples").

One of the things you will notice immediately in these examples is the power of story. We are a people of stories—actually a people whose very identity grows from the greatest story—and the question to ask ourselves as we prepare ways to help people live generous lives is, "Are we helping people see their role in the story of generosity and how it changes the world?"

Here is an example of the kind of narrative description that could be used to communicate the effectiveness of money used for missions and program.

> **Missions:** The ministry group on missions has done an excellent job providing leadership for our congregation. Our mission involvement has increased greatly in the past three years. We support H.E.L.P., a local community-based ministry offering emergency food and clothing assistance to needy families. We are beginning a second year with our thrift shop and soup kitchen. The Growing Needs Mission Center receives monthly offerings from our church. Through our Church World Service,

Africa University, and Black College Fund apportionments, we give $7,500 in support. We also contribute approximately $3,200 to the six designated United Methodist Special Sunday offerings annually. We can continue this work next year with $12,000 in support. Our hope is that we can exceed that goal by another $2,000 in order to send a representative from our church on the mission trip in July. Future plans include reaching out to our community through literacy programs for children and adults and participation in the Women's Shelter Project. For an additional $2,000, we will be able to train crisis counselors to work with the shelter and to build a library to teach men, women, and children how to read. Your faithful support of these ministries through your financial contributions helps our church grow strong in missions and outreach.

Program: The church council has reviewed our program ministries for the past year and hopes to continue providing high quality opportunities for spiritual growth, learning, and worship in the year to come. In education, we fund our curriculum and resources with $1,500 each year. The additional $1,500 we received this year allowed us to purchase new Bibles and learning center materials. We hope to do the same in the coming year, funding the church school needs and adding to our resource library. We need a television and DVD player for the church school, and we hope to purchase the Disciple Bible Study materials for a new group. We can accomplish these two things for an additional $2,500. We plan to purchase new white boards and bulletin boards for each classroom. We have received two donations toward our white boards, totaling $550. With an additional $1,000, we will be able to purchase these and the bulletin boards.

Here's an example of a Narrative Budget with pictures and graphics:

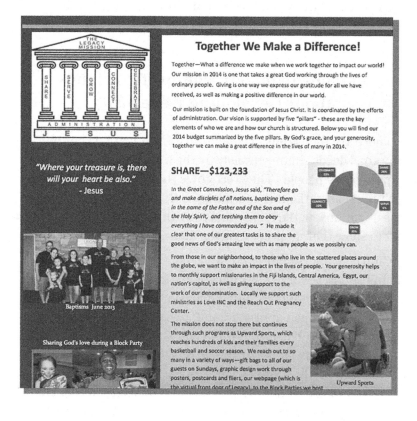

Legacy Giving

Legacy giving, or planned giving is, as eloquently defined by the Los Altos UMC (Cal-Nev Conference) as, "simply planning to make a difference, both for yourself and a cause that you believe in, through a charitable gift." Legacy giving usually allows people to make gifts designated for things for which they nurture a cherished passion. For example, one person may want to provide continuing support for the music ministry. Another might be passionate about maintaining the church grounds.

Especially given the "death tsunami" being predicted as mainline denominations continue to age, it is surprising how few congregations have any system in place for planned legacy giving. Most jurisdictional bodies have some form of foundation established to support the development of legacy giving within the local congregation. This should be part of the shift to generosity.

Lessons from our Non-profit Friends about Developing Generosity

There are thousands of community organizations out there doing good deeds financed solely by the kind-hearted donations of compassionate people. They recognize the reality that the deeds aren't possible without the funding, so they work hard to inspire those donations, make it easy and fulfilling to give, and take extra steps to show their appreciation for those who do the giving.

Church leaders could take some notes. There is a kind of bias in ministry work that infers something tawdry in making too concerted an effort to solicit donations and something tacky in showing too much appreciation for them once they're made. This is, of course, because it is our *duty* as disciples of Christ to live generous lives. It is our *responsibility* to give. Perhaps, some say, we cheapen the gospel by treating our opportunity to do God's work in the same way we treat the 'marketplace' of charitable options out there. Indeed, inspiration is a far more powerful tool than guilt. Using all the creative tools at our disposal to joyfully inspire people to generosity is, itself, responsible stewardship of the gifts we have been given. Gratitude and celebration—celebration being a joyous permutation of gratitude— are fruits of the biblically generous lifestyle.

Why are we so timid?

Secular nonprofits don't take generosity for granted. They don't settle for praying for an outcome. Obviously, many of their leaders do lots of praying at budget time, but they don't leave the future of their mission to a hoped-for miracle while they lethargically slog through the motions with their fundraising

214

campaigns. They work long and hard to achieve a goal. We ministry leaders are generally practical about most aspects of our ministry infrastructure: we don't sit around praying for the broken air conditioning to spontaneously self-repair. We call the AC guy, we pay him, and he does the job. Sure, there might be miraculous notes in that story—prayers that are answered—but the point is that we work the practical process. Same thing with planning Vacation Bible School: we plan, we prepare, we recruit, we advertise. We do everything we can to empower success. Miracles are most often born of hard work.

Why then are we so lackadaisical about stewardship?

Secular nonprofit leaders are a great source for ideas that work equally as well (but with perhaps a new perspective) in the spiritual realm. For instance, Vanessa Chase Lockshin writes on her website, *The Story Telling Non-Profit,* about a formula she has found to be a model for success:

Impact + Accountability = Great Stewardship

From the perspective of non-church-related charitable institutions, donors are most comfortable giving to institutions which are clear and transparent about where every penny is spent, and they are most inspired about giving to institutions in which their generosity makes a discernible difference. Therefore, Lockshin advises, tell donors as many stories as possible about why their donations matter, and give those donors complete confidence about the integrity with which those donations are allocated.

She offers these four perspectives on storytelling (and although she does it from a secular angle, they each have wonderful parallels for churches):

A client's success story. Tell stories from the perspective of someone who has been directly impacted by your ministry (someone who was sick and was comforted; someone who needed counseling and found hope; someone who was hungry and was fed; someone who felt lonely and discovered a welcoming community). Explain explicitly how the generosity of your faith community made those moments possible. If you can't find any examples of such stories to be told, you have a whole different set of problems on your hands.

A program staff member's story. Church staff can share inspirational stories about the work they are privileged to do and how generosity makes that work possible. Try to find interesting, unexpected insights into how lives are changed.

A volunteer's story. Those who have volunteered can share inspiring stories about how they have seen God at work (in themselves and in others) through the work they have done with your ministry teams. Make the connection between that work happening and how generosity lays the foundation for it.

A story from a fundraiser who was involved in the project. For those of us who identify as disciples of Christ, these are the moments of witness to answering God's call to stewardship—our understanding that we are merely stewards of God's blessings in this life.[9]

Build a team to develop a strategy for sharing your stories, and keep in mind the goals for helping your congregation live more full and generous lives:

- **Use specific stories to teach specific stewardship lessons** appropriate for your audience at this point in their spiritual journey. If your folks need inspiration to take a risk for their faith, share a story about risk-taking. If they need to be inspired to find the joy in generosity even in difficult circumstances, find people with those stories to share.

- **Encourage "spoon vs. ladle" thinking** (with thanks to the folks at ReImagine Generosity for that image). Here's their explanation for this perspective:[10]

After all, a spoon is for feeding yourself, but a ladle is for serving others. The "spoon" vs. "ladle" thinking illustrates a mindset that is counter culture. When we give up our spoon and pick up a ladle, we are following the example of Christ by choosing to think of others' needs ahead of our own. This kind of generosity does not come easily and always moves us beyond our comfort zone. For some, "ladle thinking" does mean writing a check; for others, it involves inviting someone into their life or taking the time to serve another person. "Ladle thinking" requires faith and dependence on Christ. The "ladle" can manifest itself in different ways, but it always involves a putting off of selfish desires and a dependence on Christ.

- **Encourage one another.** Celebrate the generosity of people in specific ways. Recognize those who serve and those who give as a regular part of worship and communications. Social media is a great tool for this! You can easily provide a means for individuals to celebrate other individuals.

- **Create inspiration, not guilt.** There is no need to downplay our responsibility as disciples to sacrificially support God's work, but this is best done through the inspiration of examples of where God's blessings result when that call is followed.

- **Connect people with the privilege of being a blessing to others.** Focus on the heart of the giver rather than the gift itself. Focus on the relationships that are forged through generosity and how those relationships grow and deepen when people live generous lives together.

- **Don't be afraid of straight talk.** Acknowledge that generosity is sometimes difficult and sometimes downright scary. This is a great opportunity for the kind of specific story sharing mentioned above. If you are honest with people about the challenge and risk, that honesty is appreciated. A great opportunity is then available for discussing risks, rewards, and the workings of faith.

- **Talk about giving of our essence rather than giving from our excess.** It is a common cultural view that we give to charitable causes out of what we have left over. Even in church circles this can carry over into an attitude of giving out of our excess blessings, but it is our privilege as leaders to help fellow disciples understand that our generosity is a fundamental part of our identity as followers of Christ. It is not a supplemental benefit of a life in Christ: it is one of the cornerstones of who we are.

- **Everybody can give.** If you're going to do a stewardship focus, get everybody involved. Get kids involved, helping them understand in simple and powerful ways how they can be generous people. Definitely get young people involved, helping them understand the practical ramifications of their purchasing decisions, the power of even small financial gifts (given their limited resources), and the profound opportunities to use their talents.

- **Use creativity** to morph ideas into tangible experiences.

   ◦ *Make a Blessings Tree.* Put a big Blessings Tree in your worship space and have people add 'leaves' on which they write the blessings in their lives and ministry.

   ◦ *Life Inventory.* Give people a tool to sit down with their families and explore how they are setting their priorities and what their goals are for the future. Writing things down and discussing them can lead to revelations and realizations.

   ◦ *Send handwritten notes.* Along with the 'stewardship package' that you send out to folks with your yearly budget appeal and prayer card, write a handwritten note thanking them for their generosity and what it means to your ministry. This is something you can even do at random times during the year! Youth can write notes giving thanks for support of the youth ministry! Children can write crayon-crafted notes giving thanks for support of the children's ministry!

   ◦ *Make special efforts to engage special supporters.* There is understandable resistance to this idea because we do not wish to show favoritism—the church has some unsavory history in this regard—but what we are talking about here is building relationships with people who have been blessed with resources that can help make vision happen. We are less queasy about focusing on these kinds of relationships with people with specific talents—we'll spend hours working with a creative team, musicians, or teachers. It is worthwhile to cultivate working relationships with those who have been blessed with financial resources, helping them understand more fully how God can make use of those blessings.

   o *Celebrate, celebrate, celebrate.* Think of every way you can to celebrate service and generosity. Have a party. Have thanks-carolers call people up to sing them a thank you song. Send a thank you gift, a little ministry memento. Put up a wall of thanksgiving. Publicly recognize those who give—you don't do this by amounts, but say, for instance, you recognize those who have been giving continuously for the past 10 years. Lots of possibilities. Google "how to thank donors" and see which ideas can be adapted from the secular world to the ministry world.

Diagnosing the Level of Generosity

In addition to the coaching questions described, there are a variety of tools available to assist the coach in determining the level of generosity offered within a congregation:

- *Real Discipleship Survey:* This survey instrument is used as both a personal growth instrument and as a tool to survey the maturity levels of the congregation in six dimensions of the discipleship journey, including generosity.[11]

- *Congregational Survey:* The measurement of giving patterns as perceived by the congregation is part of a more comprehensive survey of congregational health (included at the beginning of this chapter).[12]

- *Leadership Team Assessment:* This document, included in the e-book *Tips, Tools, and Activities for Coaching Church Leaders* is a set of questions for local church leadership teams to consider. The practices of hospitality, worship, discipleship, service, and generosity are all included.[13]

- *Readiness 360:* This unique online survey (www.readiness360.org) measures the spiritual intensity, missional alignment, dynamic relationships, and cultural openness of your congregation. Designed to serve as an indicator for readiness to multiply, this is a great resource for measuring church health.[14]

Most of these and other tools are available in our companion resource for *Shift* and *Shift 2,* called *Tips, Tools, and Activities for Coaching Church Leaders.* (See www.mc3coaching.com).

Steps for Getting Started

Conduct an Annual Stewardship Emphasis

It is common practice in most congregations to have an annual stewardship campaign. This usually is done in the fall and runs 4–6 weeks, most often ending on Thanksgiving. Some churches have found that the beginning of the year works better for them.

This is a time for focused reflection on the commitment each family/household makes to the ministry of the congregation. There are some excellent, well-established resources available to assist in developing such a focus:

- *The New Consecration Sunday Stewardship Program* by Herb Miller[15]

- *The Grow One Sunday Stewardship Program Online* by Herb Miller[16]

- *Extravagant Generosity* by Michael Reeves and Jennifer Tyler [17]

- *Committed to Christ: Six Steps to a Generous Life* by Bob Crossman.[18]

Provide Training in Biblical Financial Principles

Some great resources were noted in this chapter's section on teaching generosity. This needs to be part of the Christian

Education offered to support the discipling process. It was suggested in the "Membership to Discipleship" chapter that some form of generosity/biblical financial management be included in the core curriculum for the discipling process.

Connect Generosity to the Vision of the Congregation

People tend to be generous when they believe in the cause. One only needs to look to the outpouring of resources in support of those in need due to a natural disaster (hurricane, tornado, flood, etc.). Give them something to believe in and ask them to help make it a reality.

Practice the Ministry of the Ask

I have never considered myself a fundraiser. The thought of asking people for money made me very uncomfortable. What I discovered is that people actually enjoy the opportunity to get behind a credible cause. Ask them! Tell the story about the difference their giving will make in the community or in the lives of people. Remember that it's not about the money. It's about the difference!

Practice Transparency

It was my practice as a pastor to be as open as possible about the financial status of the congregation. Each year, the budget was distributed in worship so that everyone could see how the leadership planned to use the resources provided. Each month a financial report was made available to the congregation.

When times were tight, we held congregational meetings where the leadership shared measures being taken to live within our means.

Set Clear Expectations for Membership

In the chapter titled "Membership to Discipleship," it was suggested that congregations use a membership covenant. Part of this covenant is the expectation that those choosing to become members (join the team called to serve the community) commit to proportional giving and moving toward a tithe.

People tend to rise to the level of our expectations.

Tithe the Church Budget

The way the congregation handles its finances should be a witness to the faithfulness we seek from our members. As I work with churches across the country, I have discovered that a relatively small percentage of them tithe or give more than a tithe from the resources that are provided to serving those in the community.

My suggestion is that a church start with a commitment to a tithe, and then seek to increase the percentage of giving by 1–3% each following year. This is a significant witness to practicing what we preach.

Additional Resources on Generosity

- *Enough: Discovering Joy through Simplicity and Generosity,* Adam Hamilton, Abingdon Press, 2009.

- *Five Practices of Fruitful Congregations,* Robert Schnase, Abingdon Press, 2007.

- *Financial Peace University,* Dave Ramsey.

- *Journey to True Financial Freedom Seminar,* Crown Ministries.

Leading the Charge Without Getting Trampled

I want to close by sharing some thoughts about how to put some of the things discussed into practice in your local congregation. Having worked with many congregations related to these shifts over the past several years, I have discovered that there are some general methods that will help you move toward greater vitality and effectiveness with great support of the congregation. There are also some mistakes that will sabotage your efforts. So, the following suggestions are provided to help make the journey smoother.

Create a Sense of Urgency

As a general rule, people don't change because it makes sense. People change when it is too painful not to! This does not mean that the congregation has to be so broken that it will try anything to get better. It does mean that when people begin to see new possibilities for vitality, the current way of doing things just won't make sense any more.

One of the best ways I know of to help people see new possibilities is to LET THEM see new possibilities. If you want to give people a vision for creating a world-class process for intentional hospitality, take them to a church that is doing this well. If you want to create a vision for providing a life-changing youth ministry, visit a youth ministry that is thriving.

I'm a huge fan of learning from the successes of others. It is my experience that congregations that are doing things well love to share their story and help others achieve new levels of excellence. After all, we really are all on the same Kingdom team. With slightly less impact, providing video witnesses to effective ministries can also stimulate discussions around the possibilities.

Another approach is to share stories, or even let people experience the impact of what is not working well. In one of my appointments to a local church, our praise and worship service had reached capacity. While it had been clear to leadership for some time that we were going to need to offer another worship option (we only had one multi-purpose space) we decided to continue worshiping with one worship service in that style and keep adding chairs for a while. We had certainly reached the uncomfortably full situation!

When we began to have people leave because they couldn't find a seat or because it was too crowded for their comfort, leadership could begin to share the stories and people could connect to their own experience.

The best solution we could come up with was to add a fourth service to our Sunday morning schedule. To accommodate this, we needed to change the worship times for all the existing services. Usually one would expect this to be a very difficult proposition. In this case it was easy. Almost everyone understood why this move was necessary. Only one person wrote me a note that came through the offering plate and read, "Stupid, stupid, stupid, stupid, stupid." Many had experienced the situation first-hand and most knew the stories. It was simply time to do something different.

Invite Dialogue

I cannot overemphasize the importance of inviting people into the conversation about proposed changes. This is especially true for those who have perspectives different from your own. One of the truths about conflict is that it is not always a bad thing. Many congregations strive for what is called an "artificial harmony." I call it "death by niceness"!

If you have 10 people share their perspective on any common experience, you will get from eight to 10 differing viewpoints. This is a good thing. The differing perspectives will strengthen the final decision, and people will feel like they have been valued.

One of the keys in these discussions is to help people understand both the complexity and depth of the issues under consideration. For most things, other than the routine and mundane, there really is no absolutely clear path. As these discussions take place, it is an opportunity to move from the "What do we want?" or "What do we like?" kinds of questions to a more missional focus, like "Where is God already at work?" or "If we were to look through God's eyes, what might we see?"

Another key is to outlaw "parking lot meetings." I realize this is easier said than done. However, giving everyone the opportunity to voice opinions and being clear that only what is discussed in open forum holds any weight will go a long way toward eliminating "parking lot meetings."

Take Baby Steps and Manage the Pace

Change is easier when we are not changing everything at once. Most major changes can be broken down into smaller steps that make them more tolerable.

I have really struggled with this one! One congregation I served had installed a video projection system just prior to my arrival (and after the previous pastor had departed). Knowing the value this would bring to worship (both traditional and contemporary) I wanted to just launch into using it to its fullest capability. However, I listened to some wiser people in leadership who understood that would be too much, especially for our more traditional worship experience. So, we started by only using the screen for announcements and then rolling it up. After a few months we introduced the use of the projection system for hymns. People loved being able to see the words clearly and not having to hold a hymnal, although they had a choice to do either one since the hymn numbers were projected as well as being printed in the bulletins. A few months later we introduced using the system for prayers and the communion liturgy. After about a year, a group from the traditional service asked why they never got to experience "all the cool stuff" we were doing with the contemporary worship services (videos, images, interviews, etc.). We knew then it was time to use the system to its fullest capability!

Notice that we gave people time to recover from one change before we introduced another new thing. People need some breathing room between changes to get used to what has already been done.

Communicate Sensitively

When communicating change, people need to know: What is changing? What is NOT changing? Why are we making the change? How does this impact me?

In any change that is being made, people are going to experience a sense of loss. Acknowledge the loss openly and show respect for the past. Don't be surprised by an over-reaction and a sense of grief.

Share information over and over and over again. Help people see the continuity of the change with what really matters.

Practice the Art of Framing

Framing is an inevitable process of selective influence over the individual's perception of the meanings attributed to words or phrases. A frame defines the packaging of an element of rhetoric in such a way as to encourage certain interpretations and to discourage others.

One way to package the message when introducing some form of change is to frame it within the vision of the congregation, explaining how the change will help the congregation live more fully into the vision. Another way to frame messages includes the framing of the change within what people value. Still another is, whenever possible, to frame the change as an addition rather than a subtraction.

It is also helpful to frame the message in terms of the next chapter in the story, rather than a radical departure from the past.

In one of the congregations I served, we made the transition from celebrating communion once a month to celebrating communion in every worship experience. To do this, we talked about the connection in the early church between Word and Table. We taught about the elements of communion being a re-presentation of Christ in our midst. We highlighted the sense of the presence of Christ in our midst through the sacraments.

While communion was introduced as a weekly element

in the worship experience, we made participation voluntary. Communion was celebrated during a song/hymn following the message, with a clear connection between the message and the grace extended in communion. People were not directed to the communion table by ushers but were given the opportunity to participate if they chose or to stay seated and share in the song if that was their choice.

Everything possible was done to create a sense of a "holy moment" as people came to the table. The lights were dimmed. Candle altars were arranged at the sides of the sanctuary. The altar rail was open for people to spend time in prayer. Prayer partners were available behind the altar rails to pray with people if requested.

In the contemporary service it was an instant hit. Nearly the whole congregation began to participate immediately. For our more traditional folks, this element of worship was a bit slower to gain momentum. Fortunately, though, very few had strong objections if there were people who wanted this experience weekly.

By the time I moved to the next appointment, it was clear that the new pastor could change just about anything he or she wanted in worship—as long as it wasn't weekly communion!

Celebrate Early Wins

The change process is fueled by success. When there are successes, even small ones, take time to celebrate them. Help people see the impact of the things that are changing. This will help them to be more open to future changes and create a momentum for moving into the future.

In the Annual Conference where I served in the Center for Congregational Excellence, we had provided a couple of different processes for congregational transformation. In each case, while the process had some really good stuff, people couldn't see that any overall progress was being made. Congregations would work their way through months of learning and visioning before any difference could be seen. They were designed to get to a big strategic plan.

The problem encountered in congregation after congregation was a lack of momentum. Since all the focus was placed on the end goal—the big picture of the future—the energy for change began to wane.

As I built a new process—the process you have been reading about which is now called Shift—I broke it down into smaller steps with shorter-term goals and short-term wins. There was a remarkable difference in the way the processes were perceived. People could see that something better was being created. They could experience the difference that was being made. They could celebrate successes. It also created an energy that led to a much stronger finish when we got to the "big picture" stuff.

Just Get Started

Don't wait for the congregation to be ready or your calendar to clear before getting started. There is never an ideal time. I encourage you to simply select a shift, one that resonates with you and your leadership team, and begin addressing the "Getting Started" stuff to see where God leads.

In Summary

The shifts outlined in this book were identified as part of a years-long process of helping churches revitalize their ministries (including incorporating all the new things we have learned into this second edition). These ideas were formulated in partnership with many gifted leaders. They have been refined in practice and tested in diverse settings. The concepts have been utilized in every corner of the United States, by various denominations, by churches facing demographic and economic upheaval and uncertain futures, as well as churches that want to be proactive in keeping their outlook fresh and their ministry vital.

These ideas work. They work because, although they may be organized in a fresh and easily digestible way, they are time-tested, biblically faithful, and true to our rich heritage as followers of Jesus. They work because they are collaborative. They call for leaders to come together in prayer and conversation, to hold one another accountable to measurable progress.

When we are thoughtful, when we are prayerful, when we are collaborative—showing fidelity to the ways that Jesus showed us how to do ministry—the Holy Spirit always works in surprising ways. That is why these strategies will work for you, too.

We at Excellence in Ministry Coaching travel the country personally leading workshops and seminars that help congregational leaders build on the strengths of their own unique faith communities. Increasingly, we are also leveraging technology to provide distance learning and connections between leaders who are exploring this territory together. If we can help you use the resources in this book more effectively or explore other aspects of vibrant ministry more fully, don't hesitate to contact us. Our greatest blessing is working with local churches.

God bless you and the faithful work that you do!

Phil Maynard
Excellence in Ministry Coaching

Suggested Additional Resources for Coaches
Related to Leading the Charge without Getting Trampled

- *Leading Congregational Change,* Jim Herrington, Mike Bonem, and James Furr, Josey-Bass Publishers, San Francisco, CA, 2000.

- *Redeveloping the Congregation,* Mary Sellon, Daniel Smith, and Gail Grossman, Alban Institute, St. Herndon, VA, 2002.

- *Leading Change in the Congregation,* Gilbert Rendle, Alban Institute, St. Herndon, VA, 1998.

- *Managing Transitions: Making the Most of Change*, William Bridges, Da Capo Press, Cambridge, MA, 2003.

- *Leading Change,* John Kotter, Harvard Business School Press, Cambridge, MA, 1993.

Chapter Notes

Shift 1: From Fellowship to Hospitality

1. Michael Slaughter, *Momentum for Life,* Abingdon Press, Nashville, TN, 2005, p. 71.
2. Robert Schnase, *Five Practices of Fruitful Congregations,* Abingdon Press, Nashville, TN, 2007, p. 18.
3. Henry Cloud & John Townsend, *Safe People,* Zondervan, Grand Rapids, MI, 1996, pp. 21–24, 143–144.
4. Phil Maynard, *Connect!: Creating a Culture of Relationships That Matter,* 2016.
5. Doug Anderson & Michael Coyner, *The Race to Reach Out,* Abingdon Press, Nashville, TN, 2004, p.55.
6. Ibid., p. 57.
7. Jim Ozier and Fiona Hayworth, *Clip In: Risking Hospitality in Your Church,* Abingdon Press, Nashville, 2014, pp. 133-134.
8. Text in Church, textinchurch.com.
9. Rethink Church & Welcoming, United Methodist Communications, www.umcom.org.
10. Jim Ozier and Fiona Hayworth, *Clip In,* Abingdon Press, Nashville, 2014, p. 28.
11. Bob Farr, Doug Anderson, and Kay Kotan, *Get Their Name: Grow Your Church by Building New Relationships,* Abingdon Press, 2013, p. 21.
12. Ibid. p. 22.
13. *Deepening Your Effectiveness,* Dan Glover and Claudia Lavy, p. 120, Discipleship Resources, Nashville TN, 2006, p. 35.
14. Jim Ozier and Fiona Hayworth, *Clip In: Risking Hospitality in Your Church,* Abingdon Press, Nashville, 2014, p. 118.
15. Doug Anderson & Michael Coyner, *The Race to Reach Out,* Abingdon Press, Nashville, 2004, p.14.
16. Steve Sjogren, "94 Community Servant Evangelism Ideas for Your Church," Sermon Central, 2011, www.sermoncentral.com, p. 38.
17. Walk to Emmaus, The Upper Room, General Board of Discipleship, www. upperroom.org/Emmaus.
18. Alan Hirsch, *The Forgotten Ways,* Brazos Press, Grand Rapids, MI, 2006, pp. 133–134.
19. Henri Nouwen, as quoted by Eric Cooter, "21st Century Wells: Christian Community in the Third Place," Ministry Matters, March 11, 2013, www.ministrymatters.com.
20. Readiness 360, online congregational survey, 2012, www.readiness360.org.

21. Phil Maynard, "Mystery Visitor Report Form," Excellence in Ministry Coaching, 2012, www.emc3coaching.com.

22. Welcoming Congregation Training, United Methodist Communications, www.umcom.org.

23. Phil Maynard, "Real Discipleship Survey," Excellence in Ministry Coaching, 2012, www.emc3coaching.com.

24. Phil Maynard, "Congregational Survey," Excellence in Ministry Coaching, 2012, www.emc3coaching.com.

25. Phil Maynard, "Discovering the Possibilities," Excellence in Ministry Coaching, 2012, www.emc3coaching.com.

26. Phil Maynard, "Leadership Team Assessment," Excellence in Ministry Coaching, 2012, www.emc3coaching.com.

Shift 2: From Worship as an Event to Worship as a Lifestyle

1. Louie Giglio, *Wired For a Life of Worship: Student Edition of The Air I Breathe,* Multnomah Books, Colorado Springs, CO, 2006, p. 48.

2. Matt Redman, "The Heart of Worship," STLyrics, www.stlyrics.com.

3. Cathy Townley, *Missional Worship,* Chalice Press, St. Louis, MO, 2011, p. 11.

4. Kim Shockley, *Toward Vitality Research Project Final Report,* General Board of Discipleship, United Methodist Church, 2012.

5. United Methodist Television, United Methodist Communications, www.umcom.org.

6. George Barna, *Growing True Disciples: New Strategies for Producing Genuine Followers of Christ,* WaterBrook Press, Colorado Springs, CO, 2001, p. 59.

7. Dr. Bernice McCarthy, 4MAT, About Learning Inc., www.aboutlearning.com.

8. Tom Bandy, *Worship Ways,* Abingdon Press, 2014 , p. 30.

9. Len Wilson & Jason Moore, *Taking Flight With Creativity: Worship Design Teams that Work,* Abingdon Press, Nashville, TN, 2009.

10. Phil Maynard, "Mystery Visitor Report Form," Excellence in Ministry Coaching, 2012, www.emc3coaching.com.

11. Phil Maynard, "Real Discipleship Survey," Excellence in Ministry Coaching, 2012, www.emc3coaching.com.

12. Phil Maynard, "Congregational Survey," Excellence in Ministry Coaching, 2012, www.emc3coaching.com.

13. Phil Maynard, "Discovering the Possibilities," Excellence in Ministry Coaching, 2012, www.emc3coaching.com.

14. Phil Maynard, "Leadership Team Assessment Audit," Excellence in Ministry Coaching, 2012, www.emc3coaching.com.

15. Phil Maynard, "Worship Survey," Excellence in Ministry Coaching, 2012, www.emc3coaching.com.

16. Dave Ferguson, Jon Ferguson, & Eric Bramlett, The Big Idea, Zondervan, Grand Rapids, MI, 2007, pp. 17–18.

Shift 3: From Membership to Discipleship

1. The *Book of Discipline* of the United Methodist Church—2012, The United Methodist Publishing House, Nashville, TN, 2012, p. 91.

2. Greg Ogden, *Transforming Discipleship: Making Disciples a Few at a Time,* IVP Books, Downers Grove, IL, 2003, pp.42–46.

3. Rick Rusaw & Eric Swanson, *The Externally Focused Church,* Group Publishing, Loveland, CO, 2004, p.141.

4. David Kinnaman & Gabe Lyons, *UnChristian,* Baker Books, Grand Rapids, MI, 2007, p. 28.

5. Jim Putman, *Real Life Discipleship: Building Churches that Make Disciples,* NavPress, Colorado Springs, CO, 2010, p.43.

6. Greg L. Hawkins & Cally Parkinson, *Move: What 1,000 Churches Reveal About Spiritual Growth,* Zondervan, Grand Rapids, MI, 2011, p.34.

7. Ibid., p. 55.

8. Ibid., p. 94.

9. *The Upper Room Daily Devotional Guide,* The Upper Room, General Board of Discipleship, United Methodist Church, www.upperroom.org

10. Phil Maynard, "Real Discipleship Survey," Excellence in Ministry Coaching, 2012, www.emc3coaching.com.

11. Phil Maynard, "Congregational Survey," Excellence in Ministry Coaching, 2012, www.emc3coaching.com.

12. Phil Maynard, "Leadership Team Assessment," Excellence in Ministry Coaching, 2012, www.emc3coaching.com.

13. Phil Maynard, *Foundations,* Excellence in Ministry Coaching 2014.

14. Phil Maynard, "Creating a Discipleship Pathway," Excellence in Ministry Coaching, 2012, www.emc3coaching.com.

Shift 4: From "Serve Us" to Service

1. Rick Rusaw and Eric Swanson. *The Externally Focused Church,* Group Publishing, 2004, p. 140.

2. Lovett Weems, *Leadership in the Wesleyan Spirit,* Abingdon Press, Nashville, TN, 1999, pp. 37–38

3. Kim Shockley, *Toward Vitality Research Project Final Report,* General Board of Discipleship, United Methodist Church, 2012, p. 17.

4. Rick Rusaw and Eric Swanson, *The Externally Focused Church,* Group Publishing, Loveland, CO, 2014.

5. Dr. Joseph W. Daniels, Jr. and Christine Shinn Latona, *The Power of Real: Changing Lives. Changing Churches. Changing Communities.,* Beacon of Light Resources,Washington, D.C., 2011, p. 295.

6. Rick Rusaw & Eric Swanson, *The Externally Focused Church,* Group Publishing, Loveland, CO, 2004, p. 142.

7. Erik Rees, *S.H.A.P.E.,* Zondervan, Grand Rapids, MI, 2006, pp.37–95.

8. Bruce Bugbee, Don Cousins, & Bill Hybels, *Network,* Zondervan, Grand Rapids, MI, 1994.

9. Stephen Ministries, www.stephenministries.org.

10. Rick Rusaw & Eric Swanson, *The Externally Focused Church,* Group Publishing, Loveland, CO, 2004, p. 142.

11. Ibid., pp. 165-166.

12. "Our Social Creed," http://www.umc.org/what-we-believe/our-social-creed.

13. Phil Maynard, "Real Discipleship Survey," Excellence in Ministry Coaching, 2012, www.emc3coaching.com.

14. Phil Maynard, "Congregational Survey," Excellence in Ministry Coaching, 2012, www.emc3coaching.com

15. Phil Maynard, "Leadership Team Assessment," Excellence in Ministry Coaching," 2012, www.emc3coaching.com.

16. MissionInsite, www.missioninsite.org.

17. Phil Maynard, "Community Interview Form," Excellence in Ministry Coaching, 2012, www.emc3coaching.com.

Shift 5: From "Survival Mentality" to Generosity

1. Lovett Weems, "The Coming Death Tsunami," Ministry Matters, October 5, 2011, www.ministrymatters.com.

2. Adam Hamilton, *Enough,* Abingdon Press, Nashville, TN, 2009.

3. Dan Wesley, "The American Family's Financial Turmoil," Visual Economics, April 29, 2010, http://visualeconomics.creditloan.com.

4. Dave Ramsey, Financial Peace University, www.daveramsey.com/fpu.

5. Patrick Johnson, "How to Preach on Money, Stewardship, and Generosity," Generous Church, www.generouschurch.com.

6. Kim Shockley, *Toward Vitality Research Project Final Report,* General Board of Discipleship, United Methodist Church, 2012.

7. Gary L. McIntosh and Charles Arn, *What Every Pastor Should Know: 101 Indispensable Rules of Thumb for Leading Your Church,* Baker Books, 2013, Grand Rapids MI, p. 207.

8. Discipleship Ministries of the United Methodist Church, "Developing a Narrative Budget,"/www.umcdiscipleship.org/resources/developing-a-narrative-budget.

9. *The Storytelling Non-Profit,* www.thestorytellingnonprofit.com/.

10. "16 Creative Ways to Think About Stewardship and Generosity (No Offering Plate Required)," *ReImagine Generosity,* www.thereimagine-group.com/16-creative-ways-to-think-about-stewardship-and-genero-sity-no-offering-plate-required/.

11. Philip Maynard, "Real Discipleship Survey," Excellence in Ministry Coaching, 2012, www.emc3coaching.com.

12. Philip Maynard, "Congregational Survey," Excellence in Ministry Coaching, 2012, www.emc3coaching.com.

13. Philip Maynard, "Leadership Team Assessment," Excellence in Ministry Coaching, 2012, www.emc3coaching.com.

14. Readiness 360, online congregational survey, 2012, www.readiness360.org.

15. Herb Miller, *New Consecration Sunday Stewardship Program,* Abingdon Press, Nashville, TN, 2001.

16. Herb Miller, *The Grow One Sunday Stewardship Program Online,* Abingdon Press, Nashville, TN, 1999.

17. Reeves & Tyler, *Extravagant Generosity Planning Kit,* Abingdon Press, Nashville, TN, 2011.

18. Bob Crossman, *Committed to Christ: Six Steps to a Generous Life,* Abingdon Press, Nashville, TN, 2012.

Appendix A

"One Anothers" in the New Testament

1. Love one another (John 13:34).
2. Depend on one another (Romans 12:5 amp).
3. Be devoted to one another (Romans 12:10).
4. Wash one another's feet (John 13:14).
5. Rejoice with one another (Romans 12:15, 1 Corinthians 12:26).
6. Weep with one another (Romans 12:15).
7. Live in harmony with one another (Romans 12:16).
8. Don't judge one another (Romans 14:13).
9. Accept one another (Romans 15:7).
10. Admonish one another (Colossians 3:16).
11. Greet one another (Romans 16:16).
12. Wait for one another (1 Corinthians 11:33).
13. Care for one another (1 Corinthians 12:25).
14. Serve one another (Galatians 5:13).
15. Be kind to one another (Ephesians 4:32).
16. Forgive one another (Ephesians 4:32, Colossians 3:13).
17. Be compassionate toward one another (Ephesians 4:32).
18. Encourage one another (1 Thessalonians 5:11).
19. Submit to one another (Ephesians 5:21).
20. Bear with one another (Ephesians 4:2, Colossians 3:13).
21. Stimulate love in one another (Hebrews 10:24).
22. Offer hospitality to one another (1 Peter 4:9).
23. Minister gifts to one another (1 Peter 4:10).
24. Be clothed in humility toward one another (1 Peter 5:5).
25. Don't slander one another (James 4:11).
26. Don't grumble against one another (James 5:9).
27. Confess your sins to one another (James 5:16).
28. Pray for one another (James 5:16).
29. Fellowship with one another (1 John 1:7).
30. Don't be puffed up against one another (1 Corinthians 4:6).
31. Carry one another's burdens (Galatians 6:2).
32. Honor one another (Romans 12:10).
33. Instruct one another (Romans 15:14).
34. Prefer one another (Romans 12:10).
35. Comfort one another (2 Corinthians 1:4).

"Finally, there is a resource that invites individuals and small groups into a process of discovering a maturing relationship as disciples of Jesus Christ!"

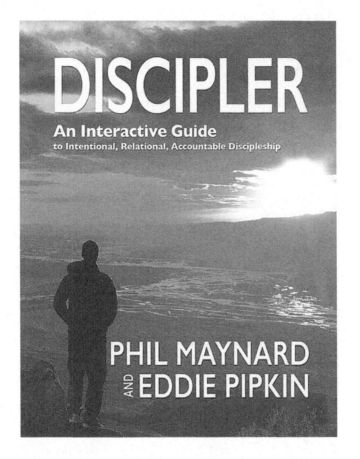

Other new titles at MarketSquareBooks.com:

Made in the USA
Monee, IL
13 February 2020

21619365R00134